PAUL

Personal Reflections Series

BETH MOORE

PAUL

90 Days on His Journey of Faith

B&H Publishing Group
Nashville, Tennessee

Paul: 90 Days on His Journey of Faith

ISBN: 978-0-8054-4934-1
B&H Publishing Group
Nashville, Tennessee
BHPublishingGroup.com

Dewey Decimal Classification: 225.92
Paul, Apostle \ Christian Life

Unless otherwise stated, all Greek word definitions used throughout this book are taken from *The Complete Word Study Dictionary: New Testament* by Spiros Zodhiates, et. al., eds. (Chattanooga, TN: AMG Publishers, 1992). Definitions marked "Strong's" are taken from *A Concise Dictionary of the Words in the Greek Testament* by James Strong (New York: The Methodist Book Concern, 1890).

Printed in the United States of America
1 2 3 4 5 6 7 8 9 14 13 12 11 10

To all those who have followed
in the footsteps of the apostle Paul,
risking life and loneliness
to take Christ's gospel to the
uttermost parts of the world

I thank my God every time I remember you. In all my prayers for all of you, I always pray with joy because of your partnership in the gospel from the first day until now, being confident of this, that he who began a good work in you will carry it on to completion until the day of Christ Jesus. . . .

I eagerly expect and hope that I will in no way be ashamed, but will have sufficient courage so that now as always Christ will be exalted in my body, whether by life or by death. For to me, to live is Christ and to die is gain.

PHILIPPIANS 1:3–6, 20–21 (NIV)

Introduction

Welcome aboard! I'm so glad you're joining me on an expedition through Scripture with the apostle Paul. Our travels will take us by land and sea to places we never dreamed we'd go. I hope you'll soon agree with me that the apostle Paul was a remarkable man. His persistence and undying passion will no doubt convince you that he truly encountered the risen Christ.

Decades after Jesus interrupted Paul's plans on the road to Damascus, the apostle's account of that event remained consistent. Something dramatically changed the life of a brilliantly devious persecutor. I pray that the same Someone will also interrupt our lives with His glorious presence as we take this journey together.

I've been a fan of the apostle Paul for years. In my estimation, his writings embody a passion for Christ that is unparalleled in the New Testament. I have accepted many of his words as a personal challenge. "I want to know Christ" has become my plea. "To live is Christ and to die is gain" has become my hope. And to borrow his words once more, "Not that I have already obtained all this . . . but I press on" (Phil. 3:12). I genuinely love Christ, and I am a fan of all those past and present who have loved Him with their whole lives.

Having admired the apostle Paul for years, I was somewhat surprised by a few comments made by people who learned I was writing a book on his life. I received questions like, "How can you, a woman, write a Bible study about a man who obviously had no tolerance for women in ministry?"

Sadly the controversy surrounding small bits of the apostle's teaching has often kept students from delving into the heart and liberating theology of the whole man. I think you're really going to like him—once you get to know him. When we've turned the last page, even if you didn't like him, you'll have to agree he loved and served his Lord with every ounce of breath and every drop of blood he had. His passion for Christ was indomitable—reason enough to study his life and be challenged by his Spirit-breathed words.

This book traces the life of the apostle Paul from his presumed childhood to his death, centering on one man's amazing ministry. If you respond to his work and writings like I did, you'll be greatly refreshed by the obvious mercy of God to allow those who have really blown it to repent and serve Him wholeheartedly and effectively. You'll also be amazed by Paul's tenacity, and through his example I think you will find encouragement to persevere in your trials. You will also become acquainted with Paul's humanity and perhaps realize he was not so unlike the rest of us—proof that God can greatly use any of us if we are fully available and readily cooperative.

I was greatly affected by the study of Paul's life in many ways. But above all, I sense like never before a quickened awareness of the personal calling God has placed on my life. I feel a renewed sense of my purpose in God's plan. I am praying for you to have the same response. You are a Christian in this present generation for a very good reason. Your life has purpose. He planned your visitation on this planet and wants to fulfill 1 Corinthians 2:9 in your life: "What no eye has seen and no ear has heard, and what has never come into a man's heart, is what God has prepared for those who love Him."

May these pages enhance your love and devotion for Christ so dramatically that He is indeed freed in your life to do more than your eyes have seen, more than your ears have heard, and more than your mind has conceived.

Allow God to do a fresh work in your life for these next ninety days. Let every journey through His Word be a new experience, a new opportunity. Invite Him to have His perfect way so you can cry out with the apostle Paul, "For to me, to live is Christ!" Beloved, when you can say these words and mean them, you have discovered life at its fullest.

Come on along. Let's get started. Today.

Day 1

One in a Long Line

Before You Begin

Read Genesis 17:1–11

Stop and Consider

"This is My covenant, which you are to keep, between Me and you and your offspring after you: Every one of your males must be circumcised." (v. 10)

You may or may not come from a family line of Christian belief. But what value do you place on religious heritage? What do we give up by living only in the present?

What role do ceremony and tradition play in your and your family's life, especially your life of faith? How have you been blessed by keeping these spiritual markers over the years?

Paul grew up in an orthodox Jewish home in a Gentile city. The Bible gives us only a few pieces of information about his upbringing, but based on these tidbits, we may draw a number of conclusions. The following narrative describes the events that most likely took place soon after his birth. The story line is fictional to help you picture the events, but the circumstances and practices are drawn from Scripture and the Jewish code of law.

"I thank Thee, O living and eternal King, Who hast mercifully restored my soul within me; Thy faithfulness is great."[1]

The words fell from his tongue while his eyes were still heavy from the night's rest. His morning prayers invited unexpected emotion this particular dawn as he soberly considered the honor that lay before him. Eight days had passed since the birth of his friend's son. Today would be the child's *Berit Milah,* an infant boy's first initiation into Judaism. He would stand beside the father at the infant's circumcision in the role of *sandek*, the Jewish godfather, assuming solemn responsibility—second only to the parents—over the child's devout religious upbringing.

He had intended to arrive first so he could assist the father with preparations, but a few members of the Minyan, a quorum of ten Jewish men, had already gathered at the door. The small house was filled with people. The father, a Pharisee and Roman citizen, was an impressive man. He was one of a few men in the community who seemed to command a certain amount of respect from both Jew and Gentile. When all had finally gathered, the ceremony began. The sandek took his place in a chair next to the father, who remained standing. The infant was placed on the sandek's knees, and the father leaned over him with greatest care to oversee the circumcision of his beloved son. He then handed the knife to the *mohel*, the most upright and expert circumcisor available in Tarsus. The father watched anxiously for the interval between the cutting of the foreskin and its actual removal. He could not help but smile as he competed with his wailing son for the attention of the quorum as he spoke the benediction, "Who hath sanctified us by His commandments and hath commanded us to bring him into the covenant of our father Abraham."[2] With the exception of the sandek, all who gathered stood for the ceremony and responded to this benediction with the words, "Just as he has been initiated into the covenant, so may he be initiated into the study of the Torah, to his nuptial [marriage] canopy, and to the performance of good deeds."[3]

> In a society where a child could be discarded as rubbish, nothing was more important to the Jew than offspring.

No one could deny the blessings of good health God had already bestowed on the infant boy. The sandek had to hold him securely between his calloused palms to keep the child from squirming completely off his lap. His tiny face was blood red, his volume at full scale. This may have been his first bout with anger, but it would not be his last. Had the ceremony not held such sober significance, the sandek might have snickered at the infant's zeal. He dared not grin, but he did wonder if God was. The child lying on his lap was yet another piece of tangible evidence that God was faithful to do as He promised. Yes, God had been faithful to a thousand generations.

The circumcision was completed but not soon enough for the master of ceremonies. The sandek cradled the child with a moment's comfort and then handed him to his father, whose voice resonated throughout the candlelit home, "His name is Saul!" A perfectly noble name for a Hebrew boy from the tribe of Benjamin, named for the first king of the chosen nation of Israel. A fine choice met with great approval. While a great feast ensued, the mother slipped the agitated infant from his father's arms and excused herself to nurse the child.

Custom demanded that the father host a feast to the limits of his wealth. A man who offered less than he could afford at his son's circumcision was entirely improper. If baby Saul's father was anything at all, he was painfully proper. Yes, this would indeed be a child well reared. "I have much to learn from the father of Saul," the sandek surmised.

Darkness was quickly falling when the sandek and his wife finally reached their home. The day had been long but the fellowship sweet. Gathered with those who feared God and worshiped Him only, he had almost forgotten this city was not their own. Tarsus, the city of the Greeks, had given birth to another Hebrew. "Dear wife," the sandek thought out loud, "our Saul seems special, does he not?"

"Dear man," she teased, "he looked like every other eight-day-old infant boy I've ever seen: mad as a wronged ruler!" They both laughed heartily. She prepared for bed as he reached for the Torah, trying to fight off the sleep quickly overtaking him. He repeated the words of the *Shema*, and then he walked over to the *mezuzah* fastened to the doorpost of the house and placed his fingers on it. He responded to the touch with the familiar words of his own father every night of his life, "The Lord is my keeper."[4] He crawled into bed and smiled once again. Then he whispered as his thoughts drifted into the night, "I still say he's special. Full of zeal, he is. Just something about him . . ."

We, too, are living inside communities of faith within a world that doesn't embrace us, or at least doesn't understand us. How do you react to this tension? Does it make you want to be more concealed about your Christian distinctions, or more open about them?

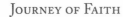

Praying God's Word Today

This means more to me than anything else, Lord—that You have chosen us for salvation through sanctification by the Spirit and through belief in the truth. You called us to this through the gospel, so that we might obtain the glory of our Lord Jesus Christ. Therefore, may we stand firm and hold to the traditions we were taught (2 Thess. 2:13–15), taking what You have begun in our hearts and living it out with faithfulness and boldness.

Day 2

Committed to Memory

BEFORE YOU BEGIN

Read Deuteronomy 6:4–9

STOP AND CONSIDER

"Bind them as a sign on your hand and let them be a symbol on your forehead. Write them on the doorposts of your house and on your gates." (vv. 8–9)

In what ways do you (or could you) keep the truth of the Scripture more readily available and accessible to you throughout the day? ______________________________

____

____

What have been some of the greatest benefits of memorizing Scripture? How has God used His internalized Word in both dramatic and everyday fashion? ______________________________

____

____

____

By the time Saul was thirteen years of age, he was considered a son of the law. He assumed all the religious responsibilities of the adult Jew. He started wearing phylacteries, called *tefillin*, during weekday morning prayers. Phylacteries were made up of two black leather cubes with long leather straps. Each cube held certain passages from the Torah written on strips of parchment. Saul wore one of the cubes on his left arm facing his heart. The other cube was placed in the center of his forehead. The leather straps on the left arm were wound precisely seven times around his arm.

The *Code of Jewish Law* prescribed that a Jewish man thirteen years or older was to put on the tefillin at the first moment in the morning when enough daylight was present to recognize a neighbor at a distance of four cubits.[5] These practices seem very strange to us perhaps, but we should appreciate their attempt to interpret Scripture as literally as they knew how.

Exodus 13:9 says the annual observance of the Feast of Unleavened Bread was to "serve as a sign for you on your hand and as a reminder on your forehead, so that the law of the Lord may be in your mouth." You can see that for the strict Jew, the phylacteries were a literal act of obedience.

The left arm was chosen because it was ordinarily the weaker. They were to wear God's Word as a banner and shield over their weakness. We don't practice the outward expression of the Jew, but we are wise to share the inward principle.

Saul would have placed the phylacteries around his forehead and arm in total silence. If interrupted while putting on the phylacteries on any given morning, he would have started the procedure all over again, repeating the appropriate benedictions. You see, a thirteen-year-old Hebrew boy could not even get out of bed in the morning without remembering to whom he belonged. As he wound the straps of the phylacteries around his head and arm, he was reminded of his binding relationship to his Creator. Soberly he assumed the responsibility of one associated with God. The law of the Lord was his life.

PRAYING GOD'S WORD TODAY

Your Word, Lord, is more desirable to me than gold—than an abundance of pure gold; and sweeter than honey—than honey dripping from the comb (Ps. 19:10). May I always stay hungry for it, while being faithful also to share its riches with others, with my children. For You have said, "Teach a youth about the way he should go; even when he is old he will not depart from it" (Prov. 22:6). Keep my family and me continually in Your Word, and keep Your Word continually in us.

Day 3

Windows and Walls

Before You Begin

Read Acts 21:37–22:3

Stop and Consider

"I am a Jewish man, born in Tarsus of Cilicia, but brought up in this city at the feet of Gamaliel, and educated according to the strict view of our patriarchal law." (v. 3)

Looking back, what are some of the things you misunderstood about Christian life and practice, things you were once adamant about but have since plastered over with grace?

Why are legalism and judgmentalism such safe havens for us? What is it about them—what do they provide us—that we keep going back for?

Although Saul's education in a Pharisee's home was probably typical, his response to this instruction was certainly atypical. We might say, "He took to it like a duck to water."

Saul was an exceptional student. Hebrew fathers were not notorious gushers, so his father probably didn't brag on him a lot. Yet he no doubt considered the wisest approach for Saul's future, not unlike a modern father looking for the best university for his gifted son. In the search for the best continuing Jewish education, he set his sights on Jerusalem, the homeland—the fountain of Jewish learning.

Mixed emotions must have filled the heart of the young man as he prepared for the journey to Jerusalem. Like most teenage boys, his emotions probably swung to the same extremes as his changing voice. Like any thirteen-year-old going so far from home, he was probably scared to death. Yet as a Jewish thirteen-year-old, he was considered a man. He packed his bags with articles foreign to us but common to the ancient Jew: prayer shawls, phylacteries, sacred writings, and customary clothing. He probably didn't gaze with affection over familiar contents in his room prior to leaving. The Jew was not given to domestic decor and did not believe in images on the walls.

All his life Saul had heard about Jerusalem. His father probably made the journey often. Three annual feasts beckoned Jewish men from near and far to the city of Zion. A proper Pharisee traveled to Jerusalem for the annual Passover Feast. Saul likely stayed home and watched over the family affairs while picturing the busy streets and solemn assemblies of the sacred city. Saul probably devoured every story his father told about Jerusalem upon his arrival home. Now it was his turn.

Most assuredly, Saul's father sought a Jewish traveling companion for his young son, someone who could provide proper supervision as the young student traveled from Tarsus to Jerusalem. As Saul boarded the boat at the docks of Tarsus, he had no idea just how familiar the nauseating heaving of a sea vessel would ultimately become to him. The boat sailed almost due south as Saul gazed at the ancient coastal cities of Sidon and Tyre in the distance. After several rather unpleasant days on board, he probably arrived at the port of

Caesarea with a chronic case of sea legs. There he exchanged rubbery limbs for the peculiar soreness of riding on the back of a beast over rough country. Thirty-five miles later, he caught the first glimpses of the city set on a hill—Jerusalem, the City of David.

> His dress and manner assured them he was a newcomer, but no heathen was he. He was one of them.

Young Saul's eyes beheld a far more cosmopolitan city than had his ancestors. Just a few decades prior to Saul's visit, Herod the Great sought the favor of the Jewish populace by rebuilding not just the temple but the entire city of Jerusalem. The desert sun danced on city walls built of Jerusalem limestone. Saul probably dismounted just before the city gate. The elders sitting at the gate looked up only long enough to notice the young traveler. No heathen was he. Noting his age, they probably nodded with approval over his father's obvious choice of further education—a budding rabbi, no doubt.

Just inside the gate, Saul cast his eyes on the impressive fruit of Herod's labors: a large theater, a palace, an amphitheater, a hippodrome for horse and chariot races, imposing fortified towers, and perfectly blended architecture. But all this paled in comparison to the structure on top of the hill—Herod's temple. Herod rebuilt the temple bigger and better than its predecessor. Huge, richly ornamented white stones mounted one upon another created a lavish feast for the eyes. Young Saul witnessed one of the most magnificent buildings in the entire world.

Saul probably ran up the main street of Jerusalem to the house of the Lord. He surely conjured up pictures of King David dancing down that very street. He hurried up the many stairs to greet magnificent porches surrounding the entire enclosure. Then he walked to a wall, one that held tremendous significance for the Jew, but one that would hold far more significance for a Jew who would ultimately become the world's most renowned missionary to the Gentiles.

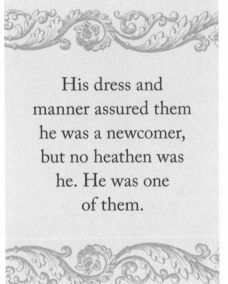

When, from a prison cell in Ephesus, Paul wrote that Christ had broken down the wall that separates Jew and Gentile, the apostle was not simply referring to a figurative wall of partition. He was referring to an imposing structure he had faced on the temple grounds as an adolescent many years before. Being raised in a Gentile city, young Saul had no problem reading the notices inscribed in Greek and Latin. This literal middle wall of partition in the temple forbade access of the defiling heathen into the inner sanctuaries of the house of God. As a young man born into a position of religious privilege, he stood a little taller—chest a little broader—as he read those words. What a contrast of emotions he would feel many years later as he came to despise the prejudice of those who would not recognize the walls crumbled by the cross. To them Saul would write, "For he is our peace, who hath made both [Jew and Gentile] one, and hath broken down the middle wall of partition between us" (Eph. 2:14 KJV).

Even with your clear understanding that God has accepted you by grace through faith, do you still find yourself appealing to Him on the basis of your good works and best efforts? How can freedom in Christ coexist with a zealously disciplined lifestyle?

Praying God's Word Today

As Your Word says, "If we have known Christ in a purely human way, yet now we no longer know Him like that. Therefore if anyone is in Christ, there is a new creation; old things have passed away, and look, new things have come. Now everything is from God, who reconciled us to Himself through Christ and gave us the ministry of reconciliation" (2 Cor. 5:16–18). Help me not to see You through the lens of legalism, nor others through the lens of judgment. Help me instead to experience the reality of being a new creation.

Day 4

Nothing Wasted

BEFORE YOU BEGIN

Read Acts 5:27–42

STOP AND CONSIDER

Gamaliel, a teacher of the law who was respected by all the people . . . said to them, "Men of Israel, be careful about what you're going to do to these men." (vv. 34–35)

Who are some of the people that have had the greatest influence on your life, and what do you most respect about them? ______________________________

Name one or two of the best pieces of godly advice you've ever received. What has God enabled you to do (or protected you from doing) as a result of knowing and applying this?

One of the most wonderful concepts in the Word of God concerns the plan He has for our lives. In Galatians 1:15, Paul described God as the One "who from my mother's womb set me apart and called me by His grace." Yes, God had a plan for Saul from birth. Nothing in the young man's life would be a waste unless he refused to let God use it.

In hindsight, then, it's no wonder that Saul took a seat in the classroom of the rabbi Gamaliel, grandson of the great Hillel—names of considerable importance in the history of Judaism. Gamaliel continues to be so highly esteemed in Judaism that even the rabbi I interviewed for this writing spoke of him with genuine familiarity. So highly revered was Gamaliel that the Jews referred to him as "the beauty of the law."[6]

All of Saul's religious training, his countless hours spent in Scripture and study, and his brilliance in spiritual matters would all be parts of God's ornate plan. God would use what Saul learned at the feet of Gamaliel, who was "clearly a remarkable man—the first to whom the title Rabban (Master) was given."[7]

He was almost liberal in comparison to many of his contemporaries. Bighearted, wise, and open-minded, Gamaliel had been raised on the teachings of his grandfather Hillel, whose words often had a remarkable similarity to the Greatest Rabboni who would ever live, Jesus Christ. "Judge not thy neighbour until thou art in his place; . . . my abasement is my exaltation; he who wishes to make a name for himself loses his name; . . . what is unpleasant to thyself that do not to thy neighbour; this is the whole Law, all else is but its exposition."[8] Do those words sound familiar? God in His wonderful wisdom made sure that the law was taught to Saul with a touch of rare grace.

God included a sample of Gamaliel's teachings in the passage you read from Acts 5. During the early days of the young church, the Jewish officials wanted to put the apostles to death, but Gamaliel advised them: "Stay away from these men and leave them alone. For if this plan or this work is of men, it will be overthrown; but if it is of God, you will not be able to overthrow them. You may even be found fighting against God" (vv. 38–39). Obviously Saul sat at the feet of one of Judaism's most grace-filled teachers.

Praying God's Word Today

Lord, Your Word says, "Knowledge inflates with pride, but love builds up. If anyone thinks he knows anything, he does not yet know it as he ought to know it. But if anyone loves God, he is known by Him" (1 Cor. 8:1–3). May I not just study Your Word to learn things and accumulate insights, but rather to know You and increase my love for You. I want the full benefit of what Your Word can teach me. May nothing—may *nothing*—be wasted!

Day 5

You Don't Mean It

Before You Begin

Read Matthew 23:1–36

Stop and Consider

"Woe to you, scribes and Pharisees, hypocrites! You clean the outside of the cup and dish, but inside they are full of greed and self-indulgence!" (v. 25)

How do you think Paul responded to the hypocrisy of the Jews in Jerusalem? How have you reacted in similar situations? ______

In what ways have you been disillusioned by Christians? How would you counsel someone who came to you confessing these types of feelings and disappointments?

Paul's father entrusted him to the finest rabbinic school, but he was not there alone. He was surrounded by good and bad influences. He saw people who were the real thing, and he saw people who were religious frauds.

We need look no further than the Word of God to see many of the influences Saul encountered among the Pharisees of Jerusalem. Saul was a contemporary of Jesus. Soon after Saul finished his education in Jerusalem and presumably headed back to Tarsus, John the Baptist began to "prepare the way for the Lord" (Matt. 3:3). In no time at all, Jesus was on the scene, teaching in the same synagogue where Saul had recently stood. Saul found influences like the wise teacher Gamaliel, but he also experienced influences like the ones Jesus so aptly described in the Gospels. In fact, many of the Pharisees and members of the Sanhedrin whom Christ encountered were Saul's instructors or classmates.

The term *Pharisee* was meant to represent genuine piety and deep devotion to God. Although exceptions certainly existed among the Pharisees, in the days of Jesus and Saul the term had become synonymous with hypocrisy and cynicism.

Matthew 23 is an entire discourse addressed to the teachers of the law and Pharisees. I hope you've taken the time to read the chapter carefully. Notice all the specific ways Jesus described the same people Saul encountered in Jerusalem. When I did this, I made a list. For example, I didn't just note that they were hypocritical, but described the *ways* they were hypocritical. My list looked something like this: they made demands of others that they themselves did not keep (v. 4); they made their religious actions into show to impress others (v. 5); they loved to be the center of attention (v. 6); and they not only wouldn't enter the kingdom of God, they prevented others from entering (v. 13). What a horrible description.

Take a thorough look at these characteristics and the others you see in Matthew 23. Do you see any that describe you as well? Godly people are valiant people. They are people with the courage to ask God to spotlight areas of weakness, sin, and failure. Then God can strengthen, heal, and complete what is lacking.

Praying God's Word Today

Father, I know that evil people and imposters will only become worse, deceiving and being deceived. But may I continue in what I have learned and firmly believed, knowing those from whom I learned, and that from childhood I have known the sacred Scriptures, which are able to instruct us for salvation through faith in Christ Jesus, making us complete and equipped for every good work (2 Tim. 3:13–15, 17). For even if we are faithless, You remain faithful. You cannot deny Yourself (2 Tim. 2:13). Keep me ever close to Your Word, ever close to Your side, my eyes fixed only on Your sinless faithfulness.

Day 6

Soul Strangulation

BEFORE YOU BEGIN

Read Philippians 3:2–11

STOP AND CONSIDER

A Hebrew born of Hebrews; as to the law, a Pharisee; as to zeal, persecuting the church; as to the righteousness that is in the law, blameless. (vv. 5–6)

If you could summarize your life in a few short lines and thoughts, what are some of the words you would use? ______

______

______

Assuming that some of your answers reveal a few mistakes and regrets, how do you *wish* your life could be summarized? What is missing that you'd like to see added to the list?

______

______

______

Saul himself was a Pharisee and probably returned from Jerusalem to Tarsus to serve as a teacher of the law. Imagine how his thinking was influenced by his contemporaries. I believe Saul had set sail to Jerusalem as a young adolescent with a pure heart; but somewhere along the way the negative influences outweighed the positive, and his purity began to erode. The law became his god. That's what happens when you take the love out of obedience. The result is the law. Without love for God and His Word, we're just trying to be good. Nothing will wear you out faster.

Have you been there? I have! Trying to obey God and serve Him before we've come to love Him can be exhausting.

Recently a friend shared a term that helps to explain what happened to the once-noble ranks of the Pharisees. The term is "identity boundaries." These are the walls we put up to separate our group from other groups. Gangs wear certain colors to show who is in and who is out. Churches and denominations develop distinctive teachings to accomplish the same goal. The first-century Jews became so obsessed with identity boundaries that they forgot their purpose. They argued endlessly about washing hands or observing the Sabbath, but they forgot about loving God.

Saul epitomized such pharisaic obsession. He packed his diploma and headed for a place to serve. Whether he divided his time between teaching and his father's business is unknown. But one thing you can count on: he was absolutely miserable. How do I know? In Philippians 3:6, he said his zeal was so great that he persecuted the church, and that his legalistic righteousness was "blameless."

We cannot begin to comprehend what Saul's life was like as he sought to live by the letter of the law because most of us do not have a Jewish background. Daily rituals determined the first words out of Saul's mouth in the morning, the way he took off his nightclothes and put on his day clothes, and how he sprinkled his hands before breakfast. He carefully avoided eating or drinking quickly and never ate while standing.

Saul pronounced numerous benedictions throughout the day. His entire day was filled with ritual, and at night he took off his shoes and garments in the prescribed order. He avoided certain sleeping positions and chose others. For the sake of his heart and liver, he probably attempted to begin the night on his left side and end the night on his right. He purposely kept his turning to a minimum. Tossing and turning through the night is misery to us, but to Saul it could have been sin!

Saul was strangled by the letter of the law. He tried to keep all the outward acts of obedience while his heart slowly eroded.

These daily rituals paled in comparison to all the laws regarding the Sabbath. Restrictions existed for almost everything. For instance, prior to the Sabbath a Pharisee cut his fingernails and toenails not in consecutive order but alternately. He then burned the nails. He avoided spitting in a place where the wind could scatter the saliva so he would not break laws concerning sowing on the Sabbath.

Do you get the general idea of what Saul's life was like as he attempted to live by the law "blamelessly"? These examples are just a few of hundreds of man-made laws. I do not cite them in order to ridicule the Jewish people. I share a few of the written traditions with you to point out man's overwhelming tendency to tax God's instruction. The Sabbath observance could not have been further from God's intent by the time Christ "became flesh and took up residence among us" (John 1:14). The day of rest was hardly recognizable to the One who ordained it.

Saul was strangled by the letter of the law. He tried desperately to keep all the outward acts of obedience while his heart slowly eroded. Saul gradually became the model for Isaiah 29:13: "These people approach Me with their mouths to honor Me with lip-service, yet their hearts are far from Me, and their worship consists of man-made rules learned by rote." Inevitably, Saul's faraway heart would turn to faraway actions.

Oh, God, forgive us when we act like modern-day Pharisees. Convict us at the very moment of our departure from the law of love You have written on our hearts. Give us hearts of devotion, not heads full of religion.

As we prepare for Paul's emergence on the biblical stage, take an extended moment to search your heart for any holdouts of man-made law-abiding. Measure its size and weight, the heavy toll of bondage it hangs over your head each day. Commit with God's help to throw off its suffocating shackles, choosing instead to both give and receive His grace.

Praying God's Word Today

I pray today with Paul, "Everything that was a gain to me, I have considered to be a loss because of Christ. More than that, I also consider everything to be a loss in view of the surpassing value of knowing Christ Jesus my Lord. Because of Him I have suffered the loss of all things and consider them filth, so that I may gain Christ and be found in Him, not having a righteousness of my own from the law, but one that is through faith in Christ—the righteousness from God based on faith. My goal is to know Him and the power of His resurrection and the fellowship of His sufferings, being conformed to His death, assuming that I will somehow reach the resurrection from among the dead" (Phil. 3:7–11).

Day 7

Initial Witness

Before You Begin

Read Acts 6:8–15

Stop and Consider

Some from Cilicia and Asia came forward and disputed with Stephen. But they were unable to stand up against the wisdom and the Spirit by whom he spoke. (vv. 9–10)

What was it about Stephen, do you think, that so infuriated the religious leadership of Jerusalem and the surrounding regions? ______________________________

____

____

We enjoy being liked by as many friends as possible. But what does it perhaps say about us if we don't have any enemies at all, no one who is ever at least somewhat offended by us?

____

____

____

No messenger could run quickly enough to satisfy Saul's curiosity about events in Jerusalem. I suspect he kept abreast of the growing menace facing his fellow Pharisees. Finally the sightings of Jesus ceased, but His followers circulated a preposterous account of His ascending into the heavens. The Pharisees really didn't care how He left. They were just glad He was gone. "If only we'd come up with that body," they must have fretted. You can be sure students and teachers debated every conceivable theory.

A few no doubt wondered, "What if Jesus really did come back from the dead?" After all, they remembered that unfortunate Lazarus incident. How convenient it would have been for the Pharisees if the stir had simply died down. Instead, as the months passed, the number of Jesus' followers grew, as did their boldness.

Saul was probably disgusted over the way the Pharisees had mishandled the problem. If he wanted it done right, he'd obviously have to do it himself. So Saul packed his things and headed for Jerusalem, salivating for the chance to be the hero. Saul arrived in Jerusalem just in time to hear an infuriating speech from a man named Stephen.

Acts 6:8 says Stephen was a man full of God's grace and power who "was performing great wonders and signs among the people." When Saul arrived, his fellow Jews were trying to debate the follower of Christ, but Stephen's passionate love for Jesus was tying a group of empty, legalistic Pharisees in knots.

Many of us remember our own agony of emptiness. And right here on earth's miserable sod, Stephen was full—not just because he'd accepted Jesus as Savior, but because he had surrendered his whole life to Christ's will and purpose. The more Stephen poured out his life for Christ, the more Christ poured His life into Stephen.

Stephen was full of faith, full of God's grace and power. Only a person full of the Holy Spirit can possess the kind of power Stephen displayed and yet remain full of God's grace. You see, a person full of the Holy Spirit cannot be full of self. Pride never accompanies power in the fully yielded life.

Stephen showed biblical meekness—the power of God in a loving package—but his witness infuriated Saul's fellow Jews. So they cooked up some false charges against Stephen, much as they had against Jesus.

> The seed might take a while to germinate, but the rabbi from Tarsus would never escape the witness of Stephen.

They brought Stephen before the Sanhedrin and confronted him with false witnesses. When those sitting in the Sanhedrin looked at Stephen, they got a shock. "His face was like the face of an angel" (Acts 6:15).

I wonder if they thought of Moses. Scripture says when he came down from Mount Sinai, "his face shone as a result of his speaking with the Lord" (Exod. 34:29). Or did they recognize the marks of wisdom as indicated by King Solomon: "A man's wisdom brightens his face, and the sternness of his face is changed"? (Eccles. 8:1).

Whatever the Jewish leaders thought, I doubt they expected what they got next. Stephen stood accused. His life literally hung in the balance. But instead of placating his accusers or defending himself, Stephen preached one of the most classic sermons in history. He rehearsed his and their Jewish history, showing at every point how God had prepared for and sent His Son. Read Acts 7:1–53, and you can join Saul in the crowd as he listened to Stephen's speech before the Sanhedrin.

Obviously Stephen was not playing the part of a politician. He referred to those in his audience as "stiff-necked" with "uncircumcised hearts and ears" (v. 51). Finally they covered their ears, dragged him out of the city, and began to stone him.

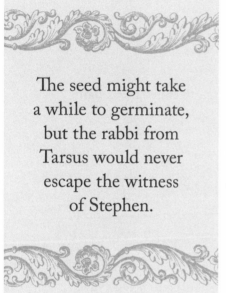

Before we leave Stephen, don't miss a final detail that may have planted the seed of the gospel even in a zealous young Pharisee's heart. While they were stoning him, Stephen cried out, "Lord, do not hold this sin against them" (Acts 7:60). As we walk through the ministry of Paul the apostle, remember the forgiveness voiced by a dying believer. In a human sense, that one sentence may have borne more fruit than any from that day to this. Stephen's words of forgiveness were to have a permanent impact on Saul. The seed might have taken a while to germinate, but the rabbi from Tarsus would never escape the witness of Stephen.

When I think of my life, I think of all the Christians whose witness has shaped me. When I get to heaven, I know I want first to see my Savior, but when I've spent a few centuries at His feet, I wonder who else I'll want to see. I'd like to take a basin and a towel to wash the feet of those who have meant so much to me here. I think Stephen has a high place on the "wash list" of Saul of Tarsus.

What opportunities have you been given recently to profess the goodness and faithfulness of God? How have you handled these situations? How can you be better prepared next time to declare your witness of Him with more natural assurance?

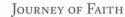

PRAYING GOD'S WORD TODAY

Lord Jesus, You have told us that our trying times of persecution are opportunities for us to bear witness to Your name. Fill us with the faith to know that when these moments arise, You will give us such words and a wisdom that none of our adversaries will be able to resist or contradict. Even when betrayed by parents, brothers, relatives, and friends—hated because of Your name—we know that not a hair of our head will be lost (Luke 21:12–18), not without accomplishing Your will and advancing Your glory.

Day 8

Seen at the Crime

Before You Begin

Read Acts 7:54–8:1

Stop and Consider

They threw [Stephen] out of the city and began to stone him.
And the witnesses laid their robes at the feet of a young man named Saul. (v. 58)

Are there some issues in our families, our churches, and our culture at large that we as Christians often approve of by our silence? ______________________

____

____

Not that Saul was uncomfortable being counted as one of this mob, but in what ways do you find yourself influenced by group dynamics and peer pressure, even as a grown-up?

____

____

____

The Bible mentions Saul for the first time in Acts 7:58. "The witnesses laid their robes at the feet of a young man named Saul." Remember him in this role of coat-watcher, because it's the last time you'll see it. Saul's zeal quickly took him on to active persecution of the followers of Jesus.

Yes, Saul was there, giving approval to Stephen's death. The original Greek word for approval is *suneudokeo*. Are you ready for this? It means "to take pleasure with others." It is a word sometimes used of both parties in a marriage who are mutually pleased with something (see 1 Cor. 7:12–13). Applying the original meaning to Saul's actions, the scene becomes clearer. He was pleased with their actions, and they were pleased with his approval. A mutual admiration society. To provide further startling clarity, consider that the verb tense of the word describing Saul's action expresses continuous or repeated action. In other words, Saul was virtually cheering throughout the entire exhibit. He didn't just give his approval when Stephen breathed his last. He cheered at every blow, like points on a scoreboard.

As Jesus watched, He didn't miss a single nod of Saul's phylacteried head. Remember, Christ was up on His feet at the time (see v. 56). Can you imagine the alloy of emotions He must have experienced as He looked on the two key players in the kingdom that day? One *for* Him; one *against* Him. One covered in blood; the other covered by prayer shawls. One who could not save himself from men; the other who could not save himself from sin. One dead in body but alive in spirit; the other alive in body but dead in spirit. One loved by God; and the other loved by God. Grace, grace, God's grace.

Just a day in the life of a man named Stephen. A shooting star. He had one brief performance. One chance on stage. But it was absolutely unforgettable. As the curtain fell on his life, he received a standing ovation from the only One who really mattered. I have a feeling that seconds later the two of them hadn't changed positions much. Christ was still on His feet. Stephen was still crumpled to his knees. How sweet to imagine the first heavenly words he heard that day: "Welcome, Stephanos, My joy and My crown."

Praying God's Word Today

Father, may we not be conformed to this age, but be transformed by the renewing of our minds, so that we may discern Your good, pleasing, and perfect will (Rom. 12:2). As You have said in Your Word, "Blessed is the man who does not condemn himself by what he approves" (Rom. 14:22). May my actions and attitudes bear witness to the indwelling character of Christ within me.

Day 9

Fade to Gray

Before You Begin

Read Acts 9:1–9

Stop and Consider

Saul got up from the ground, and though his eyes were open, he could see nothing. So they took him by the hand and led him into Damascus. (v. 8)

Interesting, isn't it, that Saul wasn't searching for Jesus at the moment of his conversion. What does that tell you about the pursuing love of Christ? ____________________

Your saving encounter with Jesus may very likely have come with fewer flashes of light than Saul's did. Has this troubled you? Why should it not? ____________________

If you asked me today what I question most at this point in my journey with Christ, my answer would not be, "Why do bad things happen to good people?" Nor would it be, "Why have You allowed me this suffering?" It would most definitely be, "Why did You call me? With all my failures and frailties, why do I have the privilege of loving You, of knowing You the little that I do?"

As the blinding light falls suddenly on a murderous persecutor, we may be left in the dark to understand why we each have been called; but our eyes will be opened to the One who called. And we will sigh and confess, "How very like Him."

Dr. Luke's account of Saul's conversion is probably quite familiar to you. In my mind's eye I can just see young Saul strutting around Jerusalem, determined to make a name for himself as a hotheaded rabbi seeking authorization to arrest followers of Jesus in Damascus and return them to Jerusalem. He was on his journey when God intervened and knocked him off his donkey. Jesus asked Saul, "Why are you persecuting Me?" (Acts 9:4). This encounter left a blind and very chastened Saul being led into Damascus where he would hear about Jesus from a courageous believer named Ananias.

Would you agree that no example could much better illustrate the statement that a person can be sincere in his beliefs yet be sincerely wrong? Saul knew it all, and yet he knew nothing.

I remember some of my first experiences when this formerly dogmatic, closed-minded woman unwillingly discovered the shade of gray. I used to see everything in black and white. I've concluded that for those who only see gray, God often emphatically and lovingly paints portraits of black and white so they are forced to acknowledge the contrasts. For those who only see black and white, He introduces situations when answers aren't so easy, where lists "A to Z" cannot be found, and when points one, two, and three don't work. Gray.

Life is full of grays, but in Saul's dramatic conversion, you and I get to enjoy a little black and white—the evil of a sinner's heart, the purity of a Savior's mercy.

Praying God's Word Today

Lord Jesus, though You have sought and found us in various ways according to Your perfect will and knowledge, Your Spirit testifies together with our spirit that we are Your children, and if children, also heirs—heirs of God and co-heirs with Christ (Rom. 8:16–17). Far from being for our sakes alone, this causes us to praise You for Your glorious grace—the grace with which You have favored us in the Beloved (Eph. 1:6). We who deserve so little have been lavished with Your love. How can I begin to thank You?

Day 10

Change of Plans

BEFORE YOU BEGIN

Read Philippians 3:12–21

STOP AND CONSIDER

One thing I do: forgetting what is behind and reaching forward to what is ahead, I pursue as my goal the prize promised by God's heavenly call in Christ Jesus. (vv. 13–14)

Saul's life is a testimony to zeal misplaced and then transformed toward an eternal purpose. How does a sense of purpose play into the activities you perform each day?

If you're regularly suffering from a *lack* of purpose and meaning, does the problem lie with the things you're doing, or with the way you're doing them? Or both?

After such noble beginnings, such strict following of God's laws, incomparable attainment of the knowledge of Scripture, and every external mark of righteousness—what happened? How did a brilliant young rabbi become a relentless persecutor of men and women? He certainly did not develop into a murderous zealot under the instruction of Gamaliel, his highly esteemed teacher. Under similar circumstances, Gamaliel counseled his fellow leaders: "I tell you, stay away from these men and leave them alone. For if this plan or this work is of men, it will be overthrown" (Acts 5:38).

Saul was not unlike others—the young and inexperienced—those who think they have all the answers. The obvious difference is that Saul's answers were lethal. Saul thought he was smarter than his teacher. No sense in waiting to see if the people of the Way would finally dissipate. He took matters into his own hands and tried to give them a much-needed shove. Acts 26:11 describes Saul's mental state perfectly: he had become obsessed. "Many a time I went from one synagogue to another to have them punished, and I tried to force them to blaspheme. In my obsession against them, I even went to foreign cities to persecute them" (Acts 26:11 NIV).

I'm certainly no counselor, but I suspect that most obsessions rise from a futile attempt to fill a gaping hole somewhere deep in a life. Saul's external righteousness and achieved goals left behind an itch he could not scratch. Can you imagine how miserable he must have been? Religiously righteous to the bone, inside he had nothing but innately wicked marrow. All that work, and it hadn't worked. All his righteous passion turned into unrighteous zeal, and he became dangerous.

The Greek word for "obsessed" is *emmainomai*. The root word is *mainomai,* which means "to act like a maniac." Our best attempts at homegrown righteousness are still but a moment from the unspeakable. Passions can turn a new direction with frightening speed. May none of us forget it. The prophet Isaiah said, "All our righteous acts are like filthy rags" (Isa. 64:6 NIV). If all the righteousness we have is our own, it's just an act. And acts don't last very long.

In this story we also get to see the purity of a Savior's mercy. Saul himself would later say, "God proves His own love for us in that while we were still sinners Christ died for us!" (Rom. 5:8). Christ met Saul on the path to his darkest, most devious sin. For that very moment, for the depths of Saul's depravity, Christ had already died. Christ literally caught him in the act.

Saul was sincere. But sincerity means nothing when it is misdirected. His led him down the path to destruction.

Toward the end of his life, he would sit in a jail cell and write: "Not that I have already reached the goal or am already fully mature, but I make every effort to take hold of it because I also have been taken hold of by Christ Jesus" (Phil. 3:12). The Greek word translated "take hold" means "to lay hold of, seize, with eagerness, suddenness . . . the idea of eager and strenuous exertion, to grasp." Christ literally snatched Saul by the neck. This persecutor turned apostle would later write to Timothy, his son in the faith: "This saying is trustworthy and deserving of full acceptance: 'Christ Jesus came into the world to save sinners'—and I am the worst of them" (1 Tim. 1:15).

Jesus sent Saul to open the eyes of many and turn them from darkness to light so they could receive forgiveness of sins. No greater calling exists, as well as no room for pride. God's chosen servant was never more than a flashback from humility. No one can teach forgiveness like the forgiven. Thank goodness, Saul ultimately became a zealous proponent of forgiveness of sin.

Let's end with some important thoughts about zeal. In the conversion of Saul, we see demonstrated that: a) we can wholeheartedly believe in something and be wholeheartedly wrong, and b) sincerity means nothing if it is misdirected. Saul believed in his cause with all his heart, yet it led him down the path to destruction. Saul was sincere. As he stated in Acts 26:9, "I myself supposed it was necessary to do many things in opposition to the name of Jesus the Nazarene."

Christ not only snatched Saul from Satan that pivotal day; He also snatched Saul from himself—from his own misguided zeal, his own obsessions. He can snatch you from yours too. I'm living proof. I couldn't count the times during any given month that I thank God for saving me not only from Satan but from myself.

Having studied the life of Saul, how can we ever doubt that Christ can save? Is anyone too wicked? Anyone too murderous? Grace never draws a line with a willing soul. His arm is never too short to save (see Isa. 59:1). He can reach into the deepest pit or down the dustiest road to Damascus. Yes, some things are gray such as, "Why did He choose us?" But some things are still black and white—I once was lost, but now I'm found, was blind but now I see.

Of the many things Christ has saved you from, what are some of the most significant? If He hadn't come along when He did, what might you have become? Where might your doubts and determinations have led you?

PRAYING GOD'S WORD TODAY

You, Lord God, the One who created the heavens and stretched them out, who spread out the earth and what comes from it, who gives breath to the people on it and life to those who walk on it—You have called us for a righteous purpose, and You will hold us by Your hand (Isa. 42:5–6), leading us where You desire. May my desire be Yours, and may I follow faithfully, directing my zeal and passion for holy, eternal purposes.

Day 11

Noticeable Differences

BEFORE YOU BEGIN

Read Acts 9:10–25

STOP AND CONSIDER

All who heard him were astounded and said, "Isn't this the man who, in Jerusalem, was destroying those who called on this name?" (v. 21)

What changes has Christ made in your life since you put your trust in Him? Even if you received him as a child, how is He continuing to change you . . . as recently as today?

How do you react to your seemingly constant need for repentance and refinement? Does it drive you crazy? Does it discourage you? Or does it comfort you to know that He's still willing to keep working on you?

Few things are more precious than the expressions on a newborn's face as he or she is suddenly cast from the darkness of the womb into the bright lights of the delivery room. I remember both laughing and crying at my daughters' faces screwing up indignantly as if to say, "Would the same wise guy who turned on that light mind turning it off?"

Many years ago when a grown man was born again on the dusty road to Damascus, a light came on that no one was able to turn off. We will soon discover many who tried.

The Lord told Ananias to look for Saul praying at a certain house. The Bible doesn't tell us the content of Saul's prayer, but it does tell us what happened next. Ananias came to Saul, and . . .

> Then he placed his hands on him and said, "Brother Saul, the Lord Jesus, who appeared to you on the road you were traveling, has sent me so you may regain your sight and be filled with the Holy Spirit." At once something like scales fell from his eyes, and he regained his sight. Then he got up and was baptized. (Acts 9:17–18)

Paul's version of these events appears in Galatians 1:14–18. He was careful to tell the reader that he did not consult any man but went immediately into Arabia following his conversion. Apparently Saul thought he'd better get to know the One who obviously knew him so well. He had already learned more about Scripture in his young years than most learn in a lifetime. What he needed now was to come to grips with the Author.

When his quiet exile with the Savior was over, he once again approached the ancient city of Damascus. What strange thoughts must have clouded his mind. He first came to Damascus to profane the name of Christ. Now he returned to *preach* the name of Christ. He first came to Damascus to take prisoner the followers of the Way. Now he would stay in their homes. He had to know he would be the talk of the town, yet the inevitable mockery did not slow him down.

In fact, we read that "Saul grew more and more powerful and baffled the Jews living in Damascus by proving that Jesus is the Christ" (Acts 9:22 NIV). This verse tells us two wonderful things about Saul:

> They expected him to return with prisoners. Instead, only one prisoner returned: a prisoner of Jesus Christ.

1. *He grew more powerful.* The Greek word for "powerful" is *endunamoo*, also used in Hebrews 11:34 as a description of Samson. The supernatural power Samson possessed physically, God gave to Saul spiritually! Saul was probably a man of small physical stature. A writer in the second century described him as "a man rather small in size, bald-headed, bow-legged, with meeting eyebrows, a large, red and somewhat hooked nose."[9] Little about his physical appearance was intimidating, but when the Spirit of God fell on him, he became the spiritual heavyweight champion of the world!

2. *He proved to the Jews that Jesus is the Christ.* The word translated as "proved" or "proving" means "to cause to come together, to bring together . . . to join or knit together." Let's insert one of these phrases in the Scripture so we can see the picture God is drawing for us. "Saul . . . [knit together to] the Jews . . . that Jesus is the Christ" (Acts 9:22). What did he knit together? The old with the new! He knit the teachings of the Old Testament Law and Prophets with their fulfillment in Jesus Christ.

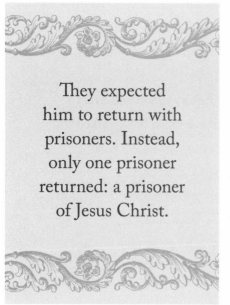

His speech to them was probably much like Christ's speech to the two travelers on the road to Emmaus. Luke tells us that Christ appeared to the men on the road, but they did not recognize him. "Then beginning with Moses and all the Prophets, He interpreted for them the things concerning Himself in all the Scriptures" (Luke 24:27). Both Christ and Saul proved He was the promised Messiah by knitting the promises of the Old Testament to their fulfillment in Jesus. The proof was there. All they needed to do was believe. Unlike the Gentiles, the Jews knew Scripture. They just hadn't recognized the One about whom the Scriptures were written!

Saul was hardly the kind of man to be ignored. Saul with the gospel was like a teenager with the radio. He kept turning up the volume. Inevitably, ironically, the Jews conspired to kill him, so Saul took the first basket out of town. According to his personal testimony in Galatians 1:18, Saul wanted to get acquainted with Peter anyway. From the look of things, this was a perfect time for a visit to Jerusalem.

Can you imagine how differently Saul must have approached the city this time? Every step he took had new significance. Damascus was northeast of Jerusalem, so Saul walked past the Mount of Olives and the Garden of Gethsemane. He walked through the Kidron Valley, dodging the hardened ground over ancient graves. He walked through the city gates where his face was recognized instantly. The chief priests expected him to return with prisoners. Instead, only one prisoner returned: a prisoner of Jesus Christ.

Are there elements of your reputation that make it hard for you (especially at work or within your family) to relinquish visible control of your life to Christ? What patterns of expected behavior present the toughest obstacles to overcome? ____________________

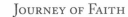

Praying God's Word Today

O Lord, place deep within my heart the desire to put it all away—anger, wrath, malice, slander, lying, filthy language—everything. For the reality is this: I have put off the old man with his practices and have put on the new man, who is being renewed in knowledge according to my Creator's image (Col. 3:8–10). As one who belongs to Christ Jesus, I have crucified the flesh with its passions and desires (Gal. 5:24). May I bear the precious fruit of this change in ever-increasing measure as You stir up obedience within me.

Day 12

The Encourager

BEFORE YOU BEGIN

Read Acts 9:26–31

STOP AND CONSIDER

Barnabas, however, took him and brought him to the apostles and explained to them how, on the road, Saul had seen the Lord, and that He had talked to him. (v. 27)

Who are some of the people that have been particularly encouraging to you at times when you were down, lonely, or just plain out of sorts? How did their encouragement help you?

____

____

How could you be an encouragement to some of the believers you know, those who are feeling weary or misunderstood? ____________________

____

____

____

God had issued Saul an undeniable apostolic calling. He probably assumed his place was with the other apostles. But when he arrived in Jerusalem and tried to associate with them, "they were all afraid of him, since they did not believe he was a disciple" (Acts 9:26). As despicable as he had been, our hearts sting for him a little, don't they? Perhaps each of us can relate to the unique stab of loneliness.

Two wonderful words begin the next verse: "But Barnabas." We will meet many people through our study. Some will be honorable. Others will not. A few will be heroes. Without a doubt Barnabas was a hero. Few things touch my heart more than Christian men who risk vulnerability in obedience to Christ. Barnabas reached out a helping hand to a discouraged man. Saul took that hand. Two lives bonded in that moment.

Barnabas offers us an example we don't want to miss. His name had been Joseph, but the disciples renamed him "son of encouragement." God used Barnabas over and over to give others the courage to be the people He had called them to be. When Barnabas brought Saul before the other apostles, they may have remembered how each of them had been the focus of his encouragement at one time or another. Now he encouraged them to accept a new brother. Many probably criticized Barnabas for being gullible concerning Saul. Barnabas was willing to give people a chance even when others weren't.

Barnabas persuaded the apostles to accept the new convert, and the most powerful preacher in all Christendom was set loose in Jerusalem. Consequently, Saul did such a fine job of debating the Grecian Jews, he nearly got himself killed. The brothers pushed Saul on a boat to Tarsus to keep him from losing his head. I can't help but chuckle at the words that follow Saul's departure: "So the church throughout all Judea, Galilee, and Samaria had peace" (Acts 9:31). Saul had a way of stirring things up. No doubt, Tarsus had enjoyed her last breath of peace for a while. Saul was on his way.

Meanwhile, the church he left behind "was strengthened; and encouraged by the Holy Spirit, it grew in numbers" (v. 31 NIV). Sounds like Barnabas still hung around awhile, doesn't it? Let's look for ways to be a Barnabas in another's life.

Praying God's Word Today

God of endurance and encouragement, I thank You for granting us agreement with other believers so that we may glorify You, the Father of our Lord Jesus Christ, with a united mind and voice (Rom. 15:5–6). With this in mind, open my eyes to new opportunities to encourage others daily, while it is still called today, so that none of us will be hardened by sin's deception. For we have truly become companions of Christ if we hold firmly until the end the reality that we had at the start (Heb. 3:13–14). Make me an encourager!

Day 13

Pride and Prejudice

Before You Begin

Read Acts 10:9–28

Stop and Consider

"You know it's forbidden for a Jewish man to associate with or visit a foreigner. But God has shown me that I must not call any person common or unclean." (v. 28)

Has God opened your mind about some form of prejudice in your life? How has he led you to correct these tendencies? What might happen if you followed through on them?

If you knew that prejudice was one of the things blocking your free flow of communication with God and His Word, how much importance would you place on removing it?

One of the main differences between Peter and Paul was the contrast in their callings. Peter was entrusted with the Jews; Saul was entrusted with the Gentiles (Gal. 2:7). I suspect that Peter often thought of Saul's calling and was relieved it wasn't his! Imagine how many times he must have thought about Saul's being called to minister to the Gentiles and thought, "Better him than me!" Saul might as well have been called to lepers. Peter may have even wondered if Saul's punishment for persecuting the church was to get the leftovers. But in no time at all, God taught Peter a very important lesson through the vision we read about in Acts 10. God always dishonors prejudice.

Peter probably not only saw himself as *different* from the Gentiles, but *better*. His attitude is nothing new. Like most of us, his prejudices were handed down through the generations. Many otherwise strong, God-serving, Bible-believing Christians are steeped in prejudice. Peter was one of those. Yet his willingness to have his closed mind pried open was testimony to his godly sincerity.

Having our minds pried open is rarely easy, but vision is rarely given to those who refuse. We are challenged to overcome prejudice on many levels, certainly not just race. Economics divide. Denominations divide. Ministries divide. Differences will always exist, but division doesn't always have to result. Although God chose Peter and Saul to minister to different groups of people, He intended for each of them to see the importance of the other in the overall vision. Saul later wrote, "He who was at work with Peter in the apostleship to the circumcised was also at work with me among the Gentiles" (Gal. 2:8). God had driven the point home to Peter through a series of visions in which He commanded, "What God has made clean, you must not call common" (Acts 10:15). Praise God that all who are in Christ have been made clean.

We must be careful to avoid spiritual elitism. Everything we are and anything we possess as believers in Christ is a gift of grace. Pure hearts before God must be cleansed from any hint of spiritual pride. We must aggressively fight the enemy when he seeks to nullify our growth and good works by making them invitations for pride and prejudice.

Praying God's Word Today

Father, I take Your clear Word as a warning when You say, "If you really carry out the royal law prescribed in Scripture, 'You shall love your neighbor as yourself,' you are doing well. But if you show favoritism, you commit sin and are convicted by the law as transgressors" (James 2:8–9). I confess my sin of letting tastes and preferences legislate my behavior toward other people equally created in Your image. May I not just realize my fault; may I act on the change in attitude.

Day 14

Season of Suffering

Before You Begin

Read 2 Corinthians 11:22–33

Stop and Consider

I faced dangers from rivers, dangers from robbers, dangers from my own people, dangers from the Gentiles, dangers in the city, dangers in the open country. (v. 26)

Have you been through seasons when it felt like the floodgates were open, when trouble was coming from all directions? What do you think God expects of us in times like these?

Having been there, what are the best ways to help others who are going through their own odysseys of suffering? Think of someone who could use your encouragement today.

After the Grecian Jews tried to kill him in Jerusalem, Saul boarded a boat for Tarsus, his homeland (see Acts 9:29–30). Through Paul's own testimony in Galatians 1:21, we know that he went to Syria and Cilicia. Five years passed between his departure to Tarsus and his next appearance in Scripture. Many scholars refer to these as the "missing years." Although we have no details of Saul's life during this time, we can be sure the inhabitants of the cities he visited didn't describe him as missing! Probably the reason the events of those five years are missing from the book of Acts is because Luke, the writer, was not an eyewitness.

But consider a few things that might have happened during the interim years. In Acts 9:16, the Lord told Ananias that He would show Saul how much he must suffer for His name. I believe God began fulfilling this prophecy almost immediately. Figuratively speaking, he was thrown into many fires during his ministry, yet few would have been any hotter than those in Tarsus. He was the local hero among the Jewish community in his hometown. Most people probably knew that Saul had left Tarsus years before for the express purpose of dealing with the followers of the Way. Now he returned as one of them. I doubt anyone threw him a homecoming party.

We have no reason to assume his father had died, yet we see no reference to his reaction to Saul's conversion. His father may have acted as if his son had never been born. Even today when a Jew from an orthodox family turns from Judaism, parents sometimes consider the defector to be dead. Some observe an event akin to a funeral. Others prefer to blot them from their lives and consider them never born. Many families do not react so harshly and permanently, yet remember—Saul's father was a Pharisee! His son's defection was a fate worse than death.

God wasn't kidding when He said Saul would suffer for His name, was He? Yet many of the perils mentioned are not recorded in the book of Acts. The most likely time these sufferings took place was during the interim period not detailed in Acts. As Saul reenters the picture, however, we should assume his life had been anything but uneventful!

Praying God's Word Today

I rejoice today that You are protecting us by Your power through faith for a salvation that is ready to be revealed in the last time, though now for a short time we have had to be distressed by various trials. May the genuineness of our faith—more valuable than gold, which perishes though refined by fire—result in praise, glory, and honor at the revelation of Jesus Christ (1 Pet. 1:5–7).

Day 15

Righteous Renegades

Before You Begin

Read Acts 11:19–26

Stop and Consider

But there were some of them, Cypriot and Cyrenian men, who came to Antioch and began speaking to the Hellenists, proclaiming the good news about the Lord Jesus. (v. 20)

What experiences have you had with people who take bold risks to share the faith of the gospel? Do they make you feel guilty? Annoyed? Suspicious? Challenged?

What kind of difference would you love to see your church make in your community? How could you be part of God's plan in following through on this desire?

Persecution scattered the early Christians as far as Phoenicia, Cyprus, and Antioch. But some gutsy believers who had traveled to Antioch broke the mold. They began to share with Gentiles also. As a result of their testimony in Antioch, "a large number who believed turned to the Lord" (Acts 11:21).

When God desires to do "a new thing" (Isa. 43:19 NIV), He purposely seeks out a few righteous renegades who don't have a problem breaking the mold! Mold-breakers are usually people who don't care much about popularity or tradition.

I have a good friend at church who is a mold-breaker. He has been used of God to help make our church a viable presence in this generation. I don't mind telling you, he has had as many enemies as friends. These men from Cyprus and Cyrene were mold-breakers too. The soil across the street from the synagogue looked awfully fertile to them—so they scattered and spoke!

I have to smile as I read the words in Acts 11:22, "The report about them reached the ears of the church in Jerusalem." Antioch was about three hundred miles north of Jerusalem, but juicy news travels faster than a speeding bullet! Barnabas was dispensed to Antioch immediately. When he arrived in Antioch, he "saw the evidence of the grace of God" (v. 23 NIV). Reality superseded rumor, and he was glad!

According to verse 23, Barnabas "encouraged all of them to remain true to the Lord with a firm resolve of the heart," to plan in advance to remain faithful to Him! I cannot overemphasize the importance of this exhortation. This principle is one I diligently sought to teach my children, to make them understand that the point of temptation or the pinnacle of pain is not the ideal time to decide whether to stick with Christ. The most effective time to resolve to obey Christ is in *advance* of difficulty. Planning to stay faithful can greatly enhance victory.

I wish I could say I always resolved in advance to "remain true to the Lord." Certainly there were times I didn't. But I finally learned the wisdom of Barnabas's good advice and have been thankful for the fruit of safety it bears. Barnabas had seen the cost of believing in Christ firsthand. He was teaching these new believers the kind of resolve that would hold up even against the threat of death. And under his faithful tutelage, a great number of people were brought to the Lord.

> God is still scattering the seeds a few righteous renegades planted in a city called Antioch.

Although Barnabas was overjoyed at the great harvest the scattered seeds had ultimately produced, these missionaries were obviously in a situation over their heads. They needed a specialist, an expert discipler. They needed Saul. And right about then, he probably needed them. Barnabas headed for Tarsus, looking for him. So for a whole year Barnabas and Saul met with the church and taught great numbers of people. What a team they must have made—Saul the teacher, Barnabas the encourager. One taught the principles of a godly life. The other assured them they could do it with God's help.

The next phrase in Acts 11:26 conjures up many emotions in me: "The disciples were first called Christians in Antioch." What a great word: *Christian*—

- An emotional word causing one man joy and another man fury—one man peace and another man turmoil.
- A dividing word unceasingly drawing a line. Either a man *is* or he is not; he is either for or against.
- A uniting word, drawing together unlikely pairs in workplaces and neighborhoods over one single bond.
- A defining word for which countless people have lived and, likewise, countless people have died.

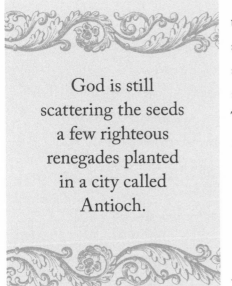

The Greek word the believers were called was *Christianos*. It does not occur in the New Testament as a name commonly used by Christians themselves. Christian was a label coined by unbelievers as a form of ridicule. Once again, how beautifully God stole the victory from Satan. The very word used as a mockery became the greatest privilege a man could boast.

The apostle Peter gave a different twist to this insult directed at believers: "If anyone suffers as a Christian, he should not be ashamed, but should glorify God with that name" (1 Pet. 4:16). Christians have been beaten, whipped, starved, humiliated, mutilated, hung, tortured, burned at the stake, crucified, and fed to lions. Yet two thousand years after a man called Jesus of Nazareth walked the streets of Jerusalem, two billion people alive on this earth today call themselves by the ever-dividing, ever-uniting word: Christian. God is still scattering the seeds a few righteous renegades planted in a city called Antioch. Had they only known what they were starting.

These who took God's Word to the streets remind us that adversity gives our faith a place to shine. What can you do to keep your faith sharp in advance of its greatest challenges? How can you ensure that struggles will not lead you to doubt but to daring deeds?

Praying God's Word Today

We are aware, Lord, that during times of hardship and cultural deception, the people who know their God will be strong and take action. Those who are wise among the people will give understanding to many (Dan. 11:32–33). May we not be those who are lulled to sleep by the times or driven to despair. May we instead be like warriors in battle trampling down the mud of the streets, fighting because You, Lord, are with us (Zech. 10:5).

Day 16

On Mission

Before You Begin

Read Acts 13:1–3

Stop and Consider

As they were ministering to the Lord and fasting, the Holy Spirit said, "Set apart for Me Barnabas and Saul for the work that I have called them to." (v. 2)

When you are just not certain what direction God is leading you, how do you go about discerning His will? What have you learned about this process by experience?

How deeply does the call to reach the nations affect your praying, your heartbeat, and your church's reason for being? How could this priority increase in intensity for you?

The first church in Antioch remains such an example to us. We've already seen willing evangelists, willing recipients, and effective discipleship revealed in the readiness of this infant church to give. Acts 13 unfolds with another mark of an effective church body: strong leadership.

Barnabas, Simeon, Lucius, Manaen, and Saul were prophets and teachers in the church. Notice that Saul was listed last of the five at this point of his ministry. These five prophets and teachers didn't just hold important positions; they each had a personal passion for God. While they were worshiping and fasting, the Holy Spirit instructed them to send Barnabas and Saul on a mission to other cities and regions, spreading the Good News into uncharted Christian territory. The leaders of the church in Antioch were constantly ready to hear from God; therefore, when He spoke, they were listening!

Again and again in Scripture we see God's perfect timing. In Galatians 1:15, the apostle explains that he was set apart from birth (about AD 10). He did not receive salvation until around AD 36. He was not set apart for his signature ministry until around AD 46. Not one minute was wasted. God was training Saul during those formative years. Meanwhile, Barnabas the encourager was proving his effectiveness among both Jews and Gentiles. When God's time came, both men were ready for the Holy Spirit to send them out. "Then, after they had fasted, prayed, and laid hands on them, they sent them off" (Acts 13:3).

I grew up in a denomination that prioritized missions and spurred a love and appreciation in my heart for missionaries. That's one reason why this Acts 13 moment is so precious to me. Meet the first international missionaries: Saul and Barnabas! Set apart to be sent off—just like so many other faithful ones who have followed in their footsteps, forsaking the securities of home and family to follow Christ anywhere. As of this writing, more than eighty thousand evangelical missionaries presently serve overseas.[10] I have no greater admiration for any group of people.

PRAYING GOD'S WORD TODAY

You say to us, "Pay attention to Me, My people, and listen to Me, My nation; for instruction will come from Me, and My justice for a light to the nations. I will bring it about quickly. My righteousness is near, My salvation appears, and My arms will bring justice to the nations. The coastlands will put their hope in Me, and they will look to My strength" (Isa. 51:4–5). Lord, I want to be part of this great work in our day, in whatever fashion You desire. "Speak, for Your servant is listening" (1 Sam. 3:10).

Day 17

Exposing the Enemy

Before You Begin

Read Acts 13:4–12

Stop and Consider

"You son of the Devil, full of all deceit and all fraud, enemy of all righteousness! Won't you ever stop perverting the straight paths of the Lord?" (v. 10)

Wow. Now *that's* calling 'em like you see 'em. Is there ever a time when we should be this direct in our rebuke of someone? Are we sometimes guilty of being too nice?

What are some methods the Devil uses to try keeping the clear message of God's Word from getting through to us? How are we to challenge and overcome these obstacles?

Next we pack our bags and join Paul on his first missionary journey! You'll soon see that the apostle's life was anything but boring. His many experiences will prove that living and moving in the center of God's will does not mean we avoid opposition. To the contrary, we often meet challenges because of our choice to follow God! Being a sold-out servant of Jesus Christ requires courage, but—praise His name—He who requires it also supplies it. Throughout this book we have the privilege of learning from the example of a man who knew opposition intimately. His key to victory was knowing the One in charge far more intimately.

Indeed, Saul met some interesting characters in his travels! He got no farther than his second stop when he met a man I'm sure he never forgot. His name was Bar-Jesus (or Elymas). He was the attendant to Sergius Paulus, the proconsul or governor of Cyprus.

Bar-Jesus committed a serious offense against both his supervisor and the kingdom of God. "The proconsul . . . summoned Barnabas and Saul and desired to hear God's message" (Acts 13:7). Bar-Jesus did everything he could to oppose them and keep the proconsul from believing. The apostle rebuked the sorcerer, and God struck him blind.

Here we read that Saul was also called Paul! What a relief! I have tried to refer to him by the name used in whatever Scriptures we were studying. But we are least familiar with his Hebrew name, Saul, and most familiar with his Roman name, Paul. The Scriptures call him Paul from this point on, and so will we.

Paul called Bar-Jesus a "son of the Devil" (Acts 13:10). He was actually using a play on words because the name Bar-Jesus in Aramaic means "son of Jesus." In effect, Paul was saying, "You're no son of Jesus. You're a son of the devil!" He not only meant the term to be taken figuratively; he meant it literally, as I hope you will see. The three descriptions given in Scripture (v. 10) support Paul's accusation against him. Consider how the following phrases Paul used apply to Elymas as well as to Satan:

• *Full of deceit.* The Greek word means "bait, metaphorically and generally fraud, guile, deceit." Remember, Bar-Jesus or Elymas was a sorcerer, which meant he was a *magus*, or presumed wise man, who "specialized in the study of astrology and enchantment."

> As we study Paul's life, we can learn to identify the works of darkness and be equipped to stand up against them.

• *Full of trickery.* The word is often used for theft achieved through "wicked schemes or plots."

• *Perverted the right ways of the Lord.* The word means "to turn or twist throughout; to distort, pervert, seduce, mislead; to turn away."

So Paul's accusation that Bar-Jesus was a "son of the Devil" was quite appropriate. You can imagine Paul came up against the schemes of the enemy many times as he sought to do the will of God. As we study his life, we too can learn to identify the works of darkness and be equipped to stand against them.

Acts 13:11 records the first miracle we see God perform through the apostle Paul. He struck Bar-Jesus blind. Satan is powerful, but he is no match for the Son of God. The proconsul "believed and was astonished at the teaching about the Lord" (Acts 13:12). This Greek definition is a favorite. The word "astonished" or "amazed" is the Greek word *ekplesso*, which means "amazed" only in the sense of knocking one out of his senses. I can't count the times God has knocked me out of my senses through something He has taught me about Himself.

God wants to amaze us with the wisdom of His Word. He wants to blow our minds and widen our vision! He wants to show us how relevant He is. How can we do our part so He can do His? Serguis Paulus, the proconsul, revealed to us a marvelous link. Ultimately he was "astonished at the teaching about the Lord" (v. 12) because he "desired to hear God's message" (v. 7). He was ready to receive, and God honored the desire of his heart!

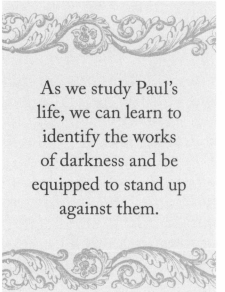

Let's learn to pray like the psalmist who said, "Open my eyes so that I may see wonderful things in Your law" (Ps. 119:18). He may just blow our minds.

Think of times you've picked up your Bible and were interrupted, distracted. How often when you attend a worship service are you distracted while preparing to go, on the way, or at the service? Does your annoyance become anger directed at a child, spouse, or friend? Our anger needs to be directed at the source. When you desire to study God's Word, Satan will do everything to distract. Ask the Holy Spirit to empower you to recognize the source of your distractions and to channel your anger where it belongs—toward the evil one.

How does it help to know that a real enemy is engaged in battle against you, an actual foe who is seeking to deceive and distract you? Rather than suffering endless pangs of guilt over your inconsistency or weakness of character, does it strengthen your muscle to know that your acts of obedience are blows against Satan's army? This is war! Wanna fight?

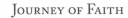

Praying God's Word Today

We heed Your call, Lord, to be sober, to be on the alert! For our adversary the Devil is prowling around like a roaring lion, looking for anyone he can devour. May we resist him, Lord, firm in the faith, knowing that the same sufferings are being experienced by our brothers in the world—knowing, too, that You, the God of all grace, who called us to Your eternal glory in Christ Jesus, will personally restore, establish, strengthen, and support us after we have suffered a little (1 Pet. 5:8–10).

Day 18

Speaking of Grace

Before You Begin

Read Acts 13:13–41

Stop and Consider

"Let it be known to you, brothers, that through this man forgiveness of sins is being proclaimed to you, and everyone who believes in Him is justified." (vv. 38–39)

Rather than guilt and compulsion, what should be our real motivations for having a word of Christian testimony ready for any occasion or opportunity? ______

Evangelism is certainly bigger than any one method or model. What are some of the ways God has uniquely gifted you to be able to share your confidence in His saving grace?

Barnabas and Paul traveled on to Pisidian Antioch (not the Antioch in Syria where believers were first called Christians). On the Sabbath they attended the synagogue worship and received a wonderful invitation. Sometimes we yearn for God to crack open a receptive door to share our faith. We scramble to grab an opportunity that never seems to come. Other times God swings open a door so quickly, we're too stunned to walk through it! God swung the door open so quickly in Pisidian Antioch that He almost blew the beard off the rabbi! Practically by the time Paul and Barnabas found a chair, they were asked to share a message of encouragement.

Paul was not about to miss a golden opportunity. Like any good orator, he shaped his style and material to fit his audience. As he stood in the synagogue, he addressed Jews and those who believed in the God of Israel. He presented the gospel by rehearsing for them their history.

I am convinced that Paul had a very specific purpose as he introduced Christ to the Jews through their own history. Remember when Paul went to Arabia after his conversion and spent some solitary time trying to sort things out? You may recall that he returned to Damascus and "baffled the Jews . . . proving that Jesus is the Christ" (Acts 9:22 NIV). As we saw earlier, the word "proving" means "knitting together." In Arabia, Paul had been knitting together the old and the new and found the two strands of yarn to be a perfect match. Paul's intention was to give the Jews in Pisidian Antioch a knitting lesson! He urged them to see how perfectly Christ knit the past with the present. They did not have to forsake their history. They just needed to accept the rest of the story!

But Paul was such a prodigy of grace, he could not preach a sermon without it. He charged the Jews with having executed their own Messiah with "no grounds" for what they did (v. 28), yet he extended the invitation to any "brothers" (v. 38)—fellow Jews—to receive forgiveness through Christ. What glorious news! If a person who had shared the responsibility for Christ's death could be forgiven, can any person be beyond forgiveness?

Praying God's Word Today

Lord Jesus, I pray that I will no longer be held captive to fear but will rather set You apart as Lord in my heart, always being ready to give a defense to anyone who asks for a reason for the hope that is in me. But may I do this with gentleness and respect, keeping my conscience clear, so that when I am accused, those who denounce my Christian life will be put to shame (1 Pet. 3:14–16). May Your grace cover all!

Day 19

Using Your Influence

Before You Begin

Read Acts 13:42–52

Stop and Consider

The Jews incited the religious women of high standing and the leading men of the city. They stirred up persecution against Paul and Barnabas and expelled them. (v. 50)

Who are some of the people that have the greatest influence on you? How have they earned the right to speak into your life? What qualifies them to be respected and reliable?

Are there others who have an influence on you for less than godly purposes? How great is their impact? Have you ever found yourself wondering if they're right and you're wrong?

Acts 13:43 shows that Paul and Barnabas's first experience in Galatia was positive. "Many of the Jews and devout proselytes" met with them after the message and received their encouragement. But although the initial reception was so positive, can Satan be far behind when God is at work? The Jewish leaders "were filled with jealousy and began to oppose what Paul was saying by insulting him" (v. 45).

This group of ancient Jews was privileged to receive the ministry of the apostle Paul himself, but in a flash they went from being subjects of ministry to being sources of opposition, inciting other men and women of influence to give additional weight and volume to their criticism. Ultimately, of course, the enemy of salvation was the one using these Jews, just as they used the leading women and men of the city. All were puppets on his strings. Little has changed. Satan still takes advantage of women and men, seizing their powers of influence for his own purposes.

I want to ask the Holy Spirit to help us with a special assignment. Meditate on your last seven days for several moments. Picture yourself in your usual roles as well as specific encounters. Think of ways you exerted the power of influence, whether rightly or wrongly. I will get you started with a few questions I am asking myself: Did you influence your spouse in a decision at work? Did you influence a friend who was upset with someone? Did you influence a class or a group of people in a meeting? Did you influence your boss or employees? Did you influence your children in situations they were in? Consider every point of influence you can remember, and add to your list as the Holy Spirit reminds you of others.

You're probably more influential than you thought. If you had lunch with friends this week, you probably influenced someone in some way. If a friend shared a problem with you, you influenced him or her somehow with your response. If you gave your opinion on a matter recently, you very likely affected someone else's. We are constantly exerting influence. Influence is a gift, a trust. We must be careful how we use it. Take heed. Satan can affect masses of followers through a few leaders.

Praying God's Word Today

Lord, help me always to speak what is consistent with sound teaching, being self-controlled, worthy of respect, sensible, and sound in faith, love, and endurance. May I be reverent in behavior, not a slanderer, not addicted to much wine, teaching what is good (Titus 2:1–3). My desire is to be someone others can trust—in the same measure that I trust in You.

Day 20

Let's Get Out of Here!

Before You Begin

Read Acts 14:1–7

Stop and Consider

When an attempt was made by both the Gentiles and Jews, with their rulers, to assault and stone them, they found out about it and fled. (vv. 5–6)

How should we determine when to trust God to protect us supernaturally and when to run for our lives? ______________________________

____

____

What causes us to doubt that this is equally God's provision? Look deep enough to define some of the miraculous components involved in using our heads. ______________________________

____

____

____

Between Paul's tenacity and Barnabas's encouragement, neither lacked motivation, even after leaving Pisidian Antioch in a cloud of dust. By the time they could see Iconium in the distance, they were spilling over with the kind of joyful anticipation that can only come from the filling of the Holy Spirit. A new challenge awaited them. Perhaps more of a challenge than they expected!

When they got to Iconium, the missionary pair again began at the synagogue. They "spoke in such a way that a great number of both Jews and Greeks believed" (Acts 14:1). But like Pisidian Antioch before, the Jewish leaders' jealousy led them to poison the minds of the people against Paul and Barnabas.

Interestingly enough, just as the Pharisees and the Herodians overcame their mutual dislike of each other to oppose Jesus, some of the Jews and Gentiles temporarily overcame their aversion to one another for a common cause. They joined in opposing the gospel message and messengers. But in spite of the opposition, Paul and Barnabas "stayed there for some time and spoke boldly, in reliance on the Lord, who testified to the message of His grace by granting that signs and wonders be performed through them" (Acts 14:3).

Then things took a dark turn for our heroes. They learned of a plot to stone them. So naturally our miracle-working pair confronted their accusers, right? Wrong.

They ran for their lives!

You may be surprised to hear that they fled in the face of the plans set against them. Shouldn't they have stayed and trusted God to guard them from attack since they were doing His will and preaching His message? Couldn't the same power used to perform signs and miracles be used to stifle their enemies?

I believe their actions offer us a fitting description of this dynamic duo: they were smart! I don't believe they were reacting out of pure fear. They were responding out of pure wisdom—and quickly! Proverbs 22:3 says that "a sensible person sees danger and takes cover, but the inexperienced keep going and are punished."

Christ Himself often chose prudence. "Jesus traveled in Galilee, since He did not want to travel in Judea because the Jews were trying to kill Him" (John 7:1). On another occasion Christ's enemies picked up stones to stone him, "but Jesus hid himself, slipping away from the temple grounds" (John 8:59 NIV).

Christ did deliver Paul and Barnabas from an evil attack. He just used their own heads and feet to do it.

No reasonable person could mistake Christ's prudence for cowardice. Look at the words of Matthew 26:1–2: "When Jesus had finished saying all this, He told His disciples, 'You know that the Passover takes place after two days, and the Son of Man will be handed over to be crucified.'"

Why didn't Christ slip out of their hands *this* time? John's gospel gives us the answer on an earlier occasion when they tried to seize Jesus: "No one laid a hand on Him because His hour had not yet come" (John 7:30). The reason Christ did not resist His accusers when they came to arrest Him was that the time had come for Him to give His life as a sacrifice for sin.

Paul and Barnabas responded to impending danger the way Christ did on several occasions. Supernatural power could have changed things. Christ could have opened the earth and commanded it to swallow His pursuers in Palestine or the pursuers of His beloved ambassadors in Iconium. Yet He chose to use another method. Christ *did* deliver Paul and Barnabas from an evil attack. He just used their heads and feet to do it! I see two general principles at work regarding miraculous intervention in the New Testament:

1. Miracles were used more often for authenticity than intervention.
2. Miracles were used most often when natural means were either not available or were not conceivable.

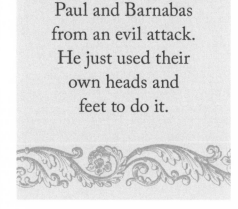

Jesus ordinarily used natural means of provision. When He and His disciples were hungry, they usually found something to eat. When they were thirsty, they went to a well and drew water to drink. He could have supplied anything they wanted supernaturally, but He chose natural means whenever available. He responded the same way to impending danger. He used His feet or sometimes a boat, and He departed.

Whether God uses natural means or supernatural means to deliver us from danger, both are divine provisions. God supplied the healthy legs that Paul and Barnabas used to flee. God provides the car we drive to the nearest public place when we're being followed. The person who walks on the scene out of nowhere and frightens off an attacker is an ambassador of God! Thank God for His natural forms of provision!

This may be a difficult concept to consider, especially if you have been attacked or injured and wonder why you weren't delivered. Tomorrow's reading will hopefully give you a measure of comfort in this regard. But for now, express your willingness to trust God even when you don't understand. How would you put that into words? ____________________

Praying God's Word Today

Your Word says, "The inexperienced believe anything, but the sensible watch their steps" (Prov. 14:15) and are "crowned with knowledge" (Prov. 14:18). May I not be afraid to use the wits and faculties You have created in me to be part of Your blessing in my life. I trust You wholeheartedly in whatever way You choose to keep Your promises, knowing that the God of old is my dwelling place, and underneath are the everlasting arms (Deut. 33:27).

Day 21

Rocky Roads

Before You Begin

Read Acts 14:8–20

Stop and Consider

When the crowds saw what Paul had done, they raised their voices, saying in the Lycaonian language, "The gods have come down to us in the form of men!" (v. 11)

How do you typically handle compliments and success? Do they sort of go to your head? What usually happens when we depend on others' positive opinions to feed our pride?

When you think of the most humble, sincere people you know, what qualities of theirs are the most admirable—the ones you'd most like to possess yourself?

Do you ever wonder why God doesn't more often perform miraculous works? Have you thought, "Just one good miracle would turn this place upside down"? If so, consider what happened here. Paul and Barnabas proceeded to the city of Lystra and began to preach the good news. There they encountered and healed a man who had been crippled from birth. Because of the miracle, the crowd began to declare: "The gods have come down to us in the form of men!" (Acts 14:11). Not exactly the result the pair desired.

The crowd brought bulls and wreaths to the city gates of Lystra to offer sacrifices to Barnabas and Paul as gods. Because of an old Greek myth, the people of Lystra were afraid not to honor Paul and Barnabas. For generations a story about two Greek gods who visited earth had circulated among the people of Lystra. The two gods were met with scorn except for one poverty-stricken couple who showed them hospitality. According to the myth, the gods cursed the people but gave the couple an opulent palace. The people of Lystra were taking no chances in case these gods had returned.

We have already seen a vital fact about Paul and Barnabas: they were smart! Now we witness a second description of both men at critical moments: they were sincere. They rushed into the crowd, tearing their clothes, declaring themselves mere men.

The sincerity of Paul and Barnabas is refreshingly obvious. They not only tore their clothes in grief because the people had made such a preposterous assumption, but they wasted no time in setting the record straight. They did not capitalize on a moment's glory. They did not use their attentions to get a good home-cooked meal. They rushed out to the crowd, shouting, "Men! Why are you doing these things? We are men also, with the same nature as you" (v. 15).

We all know that human beings are indescribably fickle. One minute we are laying palm branches in the road and crying, "Hosanna in the highest." The next minute we are crying, "Crucify Him," or, "I never knew Him." So it was with the adoring crowd at Lystra. One minute they were preparing to worship Paul and Barnabas. "Then some Jews came from Antioch and Iconium, and when they had won over the crowds and stoned Paul, they dragged him out of the city, thinking he was dead" (v. 19).

That didn't take long, did it? Think about this carefully: Barnabas and Paul could have used the crowd's wrong impression that they were gods, but they maintained their integrity. A flashy miracle at just the right time, and not one stone would have been thrown. The crowd would have bowed at their feet. Paul and Barnabas could have slipped out of town without a scratch. Instead, Paul was stoned so severely that they dragged him outside the city thinking he was dead.

> God wasn't only interested in drawing Paul out of difficulty or danger. He wanted to draw Paul closer to Himself.

Can you imagine the pictures flashing in Paul's mind with every blow of a stone? I'm sure his memory replayed Stephen's radiant face. Paul probably could not bear to think of himself worthy to die for the name of Christ in the same way. He probably fell unconscious thinking he was about to breathe his last, but this was not Paul's time.

Paul and Barnabas had arrived in Iconium with joyful anticipation, only to have to depart quickly under threat of stoning. They had escaped one of the most painful forms of punishment ever devised. They wiped their brows, gave a sigh of relief, and headed into Lystra. But before they knew what had happened, the stones were flying. They had no place to run, nowhere to hide.

Many years later Paul still remembered the events in Iconium and Lystra and shared a peculiar testimony. He said, "You, however, know all about . . . what kinds of things happened to me in Antioch, Iconium and Lystra, the persecutions I endured. Yet the Lord rescued me from all of them" (2 Tim. 3:10–11 NIV).

Any person in his or her right mind would prefer to be rescued before the first stone is thrown, not after the last! Yet Paul described both his experience in Iconium (where he departed prior to suffering) and his experience in Lystra (where he departed *after* suffering) as the Lord's divine rescue. Perhaps his inspired choice of words will intensify your appreciation of his exquisite testimony. The original word for "rescue" in 2 Timothy 3:11 is *rhuomai*, which is derived from a word meaning "to drag along the ground." *Rhuomai* means "to draw or snatch from danger, rescue, deliver." Please read the remainder of the definition with great care and meditation: "This is more with the meaning of drawing to oneself than merely rescuing from someone or something."

You see, God wasn't only interested in drawing Paul out of difficulty or danger. He wanted to draw Paul closer to Himself. Every time God delivers us, the point is ultimately to draw us closer to Himself. Whether we get to avoid pain and suffering or we must persevere in the midst of it, our deliverance comes when we're dragged from the enemy of our souls to the heart of God.

Why do you think God chooses either to work a miracle or to withhold a miracle? How have you dealt with either one or both of these experiences?

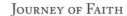

Praying God's Word Today

Like Hannah, when rejoicing over the miraculous birth of her son Samuel, may I never forget that You bring death and give life, You bring poverty and give wealth, You humble and exalt (1 Sam. 2:6–7). Or like Job, when wrought with trouble and turmoil, may I still be able to say, "The Lord gives, and the Lord takes away. Praise the name of the Lord" (Job 1:21). In any and all circumstances, may my view of You—just like my love for You—remain ever the same.

Day 22

Troubling Expectations

Before You Begin

Read Acts 14:21–22

Stop and Consider

They returned to Lystra, to Iconium, and to Antioch . . . telling them, "It is necessary to pass through many troubles on our way into the kingdom of God." (vv. 21–22)

How does this passage refute the teachings of many prosperity gospels? How would its adherents likely respond to a verse like this? ______________________________

____

____

Why is hardship inevitable in the nature of things? What does it tell us about God? What does it tell us about our world and our enemy? ______________________________

____

____

____

This next portion of Scripture unfolds in Derbe. In just a few short verses, we see Paul and Barnabas backtrack through a number of cities on their way to Syrian Antioch, where they had been commissioned. But why did they take the long route? Why in the world would they go back through Lystra (where Paul had been stoned and left for dead), Iconium (where they narrowly escaped being stoned), and Pisidian Antioch (where they were persecuted and expelled)? Acts 14:22 tells us exactly why they walked back into potential peril: to strengthen the disciples and encourage them to remain true to the faith. Paul and Barnabas considered this message about inevitable hardships such a priority that they risked everything to go back through those three cities and tell it.

Their message of encouragement by warning of hardship may seem to be a paradox to us. We may not find a message about unavoidable troubles very strengthening! But we must first recognize that the inevitable nature of hardships can motivate us to redirect our energies. *Fear* of trials sometimes depletes more energy than *facing* trials! Once we accept the inevitability of hardship, we can redirect our focus from fear of trials to faithfulness. In the face of tribulations, we often sense a heavenly strength filling our souls right on time.

Second, realizing the inevitability of hardship encourages us in the faith. I would be pretty discouraged if I thought hardships in the lives of surrendered Christians were unusual and were always signs of disobedience. Yes, hardship sometimes comes as a direct result of sin and disobedience. We usually are aware when consequences of sin have caused us deep suffering, but many other times trials have nothing at all to do with disobedience. Believing a heretical prosperity gospel can leave us terribly discouraged, wondering what we've done wrong. We wonder why we can't seem to muster enough faith to be healthy, problem free, and prosperous.

Be encouraged to know that difficulty is not a sign of immaturity or faithlessness. The Holy Spirit will do His job and let you know if you are suffering because of sin. Otherwise, remember—we must go through many hardships to enter the kingdom of God.

Praying God's Word Today

Lord Jesus, I am encouraged to know that when we endure, it brings us favor with You. For we were called to this, because You also suffered for us, leaving us an example, so that we should follow in Your steps. You did not commit sin, and no deceit was found in Your mouth; when reviled, You did not revile in return; when suffering, You did not threaten, but committed Yourself to the One who judges justly (1 Pet. 2:20–23). Grant me, Lord, to pay any price in exchange for the gift of Your hard-won salvation.

Day 23

Wisdom of the Aged

Before You Begin

Read Acts 14:23–28

Stop and Consider

When they had appointed elders in every church and prayed with fasting, they committed them to the Lord in whom they had believed. (v. 23)

Hopefully you don't consider the older generation (as some do) to be irrelevant and out of touch. How do you make deliberate efforts to benefit from the wisdom of older believers?

____

____

Describe someone who has been to you a living example of surviving hardships with victory and joy. What have you learned from him or from her? ______________________________

____

____

____

I hope we have shared some of the strength and encouragement Paul and Barnabas gave to the believers in Lystra, Iconium, and Pisidian Antioch. Those new converts saw living examples of perseverance through suffering. Paul and Barnabas departed from each city under difficult circumstances. They went out of their way to return so they could say, "We're OK! We've survived! And we're still believing and serving!" In seeing the joy and commitment of God's suffering servants, they knew they could survive too.

The time came, however, for Paul and Barnabas to leave. But they did something to ensure an ongoing strengthening and encouraging of their new disciples.

Acts 14:23 tells us they appointed elders in each church. The Greek word is *presbuteros*, which means "older, a senior." The *Holman Bible Dictionary* tells us the "elders in the Pauline churches were probably spiritual leaders and ministers, not simply a governing council."[11] Not coincidentally, Paul and Barnabas wanted to leave the new believers with ongoing strength and encouragement, so they carefully appointed elders who were not only spiritually mature but also (if I may say so gently)—old! However, older men were not the only ones charged with responsibility.

In Titus 2:3–6, Paul also charged older women, younger women, and younger men to faithful service. Sounds to me like God values the wisdom and life experience of older men and women. It also sounds to me like He chooses to use people of every age whose hearts are turned to Him.

Life is difficult. The converts in Lystra, Iconium, and Pisidian Antioch were surely strengthened and encouraged as they saw living examples of people who were surviving hardships with victory and joy. Listening to Paul and Barnabas testify must have greatly impacted their ability to endure. We don't have Paul and Barnabas, but we have hosts of older people who are more than happy to tell us about the faithfulness of God—if we'll just stop, ask them, and listen.

Praying God's Word Today

This is what You have said: "Stand by the roadways and look. Ask about the ancient paths: Which is the way to what is good? Then take it and find rest for yourselves" (Jer. 6:16). Father, may I hold on to the pattern of sound teaching that I have heard, that which has been shared in the faith and love that are in Christ Jesus (2 Tim. 1:13). I long to walk in the tried and true paths of the ages.

Day 24

Legalist Action

Before You Begin

Read Acts 15:1–21

Stop and Consider

"Why, then, are you now testing God by putting on the disciples' necks a yoke that neither our forefathers nor we have been able to bear?" (v. 10)

Would it be fair to say that we generally have higher expectations of others than we do of ourselves? How do we often show this? ______________________________

Some of us, however, place those same impossible expectations on ourselves, even higher than on others? Why is internalized legalism just as dangerous as the hypocritical kind?

Legalism. This one little word—more than any other—is probably responsible for causing more churches to die, more servants to quit, and more denominations to split. Like a leech, legalism saps the lifeblood out of its victim. It enters the door in the name of righteousness to vacuum out all the dirt and ends up vacuuming out all the spirit. Don't confuse legalism with recognition and pursuit of godly standards.

Two sets of legalists emerge in this portion of Scripture: 1) Judean visitors to Antioch who told Gentile Christians they must be circumcised to be saved, and 2) the believers in Jerusalem from the party of the Pharisees who told them they must also obey the law of Moses. The statement of the Pharisees became the basis of the Jerusalem Council.

Let's offer the legalists more grace than they offered Gentile believers. I'll assume they weren't acting out of pure meanness. But even in giving them the benefit of the doubt, I see at least three mistakes they made in behalf of the new Gentile converts.

1. *They drew a universal standard from their personal experience.* Since they had been circumcised prior to salvation, they decided everyone else should be as well. Through the ages people have struggled with the same wrong assumption based on their own personal experience. If God worked one way in their lives, any other way must be invalid. Let me illustrate with the story of two men.

The first man lives a godless, depraved life. The Spirit of God convicts him. He falls on his face, surrenders to Christ as Lord of his life. He serves faithfully and never goes back into the old patterns of sin. He becomes a preacher and boldly proclaims the message that people are not saved unless they instantly surrender their entire lives to the lordship of Christ. If they have ever fallen back, they were never saved at all.

The second man received Christ at a very early age and then fell away in rebellion for years. He returns to Christ as the penitent prodigal, slips into his old ways several times, and finally reaches freedom in Christ. In his opinion a person's state of salvation cannot in any way be judged by his actions. He believes a man can live like the devil for a season of his life and still be saved.

Both men are born again, but both men are mistakenly applying their experience to every other believer. Each of these men could find some degree of scriptural support, so who is right? God is. He is right and justified in saving whomever He pleases. There is only one way to be saved: by grace through faith in the Lord Jesus Christ (see Eph. 2:8–9). God uses many methods to draw people to Himself. He is far more creative than we want to think. Only He can judge the heart.

When we paint the picture of our salvation, we may use different colors. But in the center can only be a cross.

2. *They tried to make salvation harder than it is.* James delivered a strong exhortation to the Jerusalem Council in Acts 15:19: "We should not cause difficulties for those who turn to God from among the Gentiles." What a frightening thought! We must ask ourselves a very serious question: Do we make it difficult for people around us to turn to God? Do we have a list of rules and requirements that turns people away?

Part of the exquisite beauty of salvation is its simplicity. Any man, woman, or child can come to Christ with absolutely nothing to offer Him but simple faith—just as they are. Salvation requires nothing more than childlike faith—believing that Jesus Christ died for my sins and accepting His gift of salvation. The heart and the life sometimes turn instantaneously like the first example. Other times the heart turns instantaneously but the life adjusts a little more slowly like the second example. Let's not make salvation more difficult than it has to be.

3. *They expected of others what they could not deliver themselves.* In Acts 15:10, Peter was asking in essence, "Why are you expecting of someone else what you know you can't deliver yourself?" The question is one every believer should occasionally ask him or herself. Do we have almost impossible expectations of other people? Do we expect things of our mates we wouldn't want to have to deliver ourselves? Do we expect near perfection in

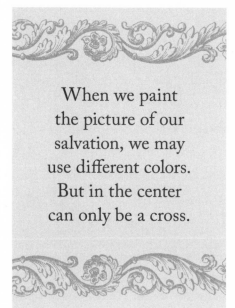

our children and tireless commitment from our coworkers? Are we yoke brokers just looking for an unsuspecting neck?

Yoke brokers are miserable people because they are never satisfied with less than perfection. Their obsession with everyone else's lack of perfection helps them keep their minds off their own. Yoke brokers are selling a yoke no one wants to buy—their own. If anyone has ever expected of you something you knew he or she couldn't do, then you have an idea how it feels to be the hapless victim of a yoke.

Let's return to the simplicity of salvation. Not adding to. Not taking away. When we paint the picture of our salvation for others to see, we may use different colors, textures, and shapes on the edges of the parchment. But in the center can only be a cross. Anything else cheapens grace and cheats the believer. Paul wasn't about to let that happen to his beloved flock.

Which of these three statements struck the strongest chord in your heart? How have you been guilty of one or all of these legalistic errors? What would change in your interactions with others if you aligned yourself rightly on these matters?

PRAYING GOD'S WORD TODAY

Father, You have made us alive with Christ even though we were dead in trespasses. By grace we are saved! You have also raised us up with Him and seated us with Him in the heavens, in Christ Jesus, so that in the coming ages You might display the immeasurable riches of Your grace in Your kindness to us in Christ Jesus. For by grace we are saved through faith, and this is not from ourselves; it is Your gift—not from works, so that no one can boast (Eph. 2:5–9). Having been liberated into such freedom, may we stand firm and never submit again to a yoke of slavery (Gal. 5:1) or be ungrateful or insecure enough to saddle anyone else with one.

Day 25

Healthy Distance

BEFORE YOU BEGIN

Read Acts 15:22–35

STOP AND CONSIDER

It was the Holy Spirit's decision—and ours—to put no greater burden on you than these necessary things. . . . If you keep yourselves from these things, you will do well. (vv. 28–29)

The Jerusalem Council mentioned several restrictions deemed beneficial to new believers. What are some restrictions you have imposed on yourself to keep compromise far away?

Why is this kind of forced behavior a necessary part of applying our Christian victory? How is abstaining from unhealthy practices distinct from the practice of pure legalism?

God can break any yoke, even those we don't realize we're wearing. Thank goodness, the message of freedom prevailed at the Jerusalem Council. Paul and Barnabas departed with a letter personalized for the Gentile believers in Antioch.

But at first glance the letter seems somewhat contradictory. Gentile believers didn't have to be circumcised to be saved, but they were urged to abstain from several practices forbidden under Jewish law. So were they free from the law or not? Yes and no. They were free from the law of Moses but not free from the life-giving laws of God. The freedom God gives is to come out and be separate from the practices of the former worldly life. The letter to the believers in Antioch was a declaration of liberty. The four areas of abstinence would help them remain free.

Let's pinpoint one of the four areas that offers an important learning opportunity for us: the believers in Antioch were told to abstain from food sacrificed to idols. Gentile believers might have reasoned that although they would not dream of sacrificing to idols anymore, what harm could be done by simply buying the leftover food at a good price after it was offered?

Satan sometimes tempts us the same way. We don't desire to go back to our old life-styles, but certain parts of it seem so harmless—some of the old friends, the old hangouts, and the old refreshments. But the elders wisely warned the early believers that nothing is harmless about the practices of the old life. Eating foods sacrificed to idols could weaken them to former practices or cause someone else to stumble.

The Gentile believers would not forfeit their gift of grace by eating foods sacrificed to idols, but they would risk their freedom and compromise their separateness. They were wise to avoid anything that would place them close enough to the vacuum to be sucked back in. Safety and freedom are found in staying so far away that you can't even hear the vacuum cleaner running.

Paul and Barnabas were now back home. Back with their beloved flock. They returned to tell them they were free . . . and to show them how they could stay that way.

Praying God's Word Today

I pray, Lord God, that You would keep our minds ready for action, being self-disciplined, our hope set completely on the grace to be brought to us at the revelation of Jesus Christ. As obedient children, may we not be conformed to the desires of our former ignorance but, as the One who called us is holy, may we also be holy in all our conduct; for You have written, "Be holy, because I am holy" (1 Pet. 1:13–16). This is my desire every hour of the day, every moment of my life.

Day 26

Divide and Multiply

BEFORE YOU BEGIN

Read Acts 15:36–38

STOP AND CONSIDER

Paul did not think it appropriate to take along this man who had deserted them in Pamphylia and had not gone on with them to the work. (v. 38)

What goes through your mind when people you greatly admire show sides of themselves you've never seen before, when they appear oh-so-human? ____________________

Have you ever made a snap judgment of someone's motives while standing on the outside looking in? Why is this so wasteful and dangerous? ____________________

Sailors speak of the call of the sea, but something stronger than the sea called Paul. He relished his days in Antioch. How beautifully the garden had grown from a few seeds scattered six years earlier! He enjoyed the privilege of returning to the same quarters every night and laughing over a meal with good friends. He busied himself with the work of a pastor. He loved these people and his partner, Barnabas. But filled with the Spirit of God, Paul felt compelled to go where the Spirit led.

We may plan to stay forever and commit with noble intentions to do one thing for the rest of our lives. But when the Spirit of God moves within us, we must move with Him or be miserable. Paul knew God had called him to Antioch only to send him out again. He had learned to obey both the abiding and the moving of the Holy Spirit. He had been allowed by God to abide in the comforts of Antioch for a season. Now the Spirit of God compelled him to move again.

I love being drawn into the story line and relationships of Scripture, but involvement also increases the disappointment when our heroes show their humanity. We are about to see how God uses flawed people like you and me.

Remember John Mark, who bailed out on Paul and Barnabas in the middle of their first missionary journey? Barnabas was one of those men willing to take a risk on a young missionary who had failed on his first attempt—the same way he had once taken a risk on a hotheaded young Pharisee who had come to Christ. Paul, on the other hand, was hard and tough. So when the two prepared to revisit the churches from their first journey, Barnabas said John goes. Paul said John stays.

John went. With Barnabas. Paul took Silas as Barnabas's replacement.

Barnabas had been the first to accept Paul and welcome him among the brothers in Jerusalem. Together they had faced the kind of peril and persecution that bonds two people for a lifetime! They were a team. So when the Holy Spirit compelled Paul to return to the towns where they had preached, he wanted his dear friend and partner to go with him. Imagine how difficult this severance must have been for them.

But they each had strong emotions about John Mark, as well as toward each other. And obviously, both of them were upset by their differing opinions. I think Paul and Barnabas were simply that different, but according to Colossians 4:10, John Mark was more than just a fellow believer to Barnabas. They were also cousins. Strong emotions can spawn sharp disagreements.

> The Spirit might have been saying yes to Barnabas and no to Paul . . . so God could divide and multiply.

But disagreements between people have a strange way of inviting observers to pick sides. I've caught myself trying to decide who was right and who was wrong. I feel a strange need to make up my mind and get in one camp or the other. But let's start becoming aware of our tendency to get involved (at least emotionally) as judge and jury when people disagree. Next time we're in a similar situation, perhaps we should ask ourselves, Does someone always have to be right and another wrong?

Paul and Barnabas both were Spirit-filled servants of God, yet they differed vehemently on whether John Mark should join them. We might assume that either Paul or Barnabas was not under the leadership of the Holy Spirit; after all, the Spirit could not possess two opinions. Or could He? I believe both men could have been under the direct influence of the Holy Spirit and yet still have differed. How? The Holy Spirit might have been saying yes to Barnabas and no to Paul. He might have wanted Barnabas, not Paul, to take John Mark. Why? So God could divide and multiply. Paul had matured so effectively under Barnabas's help and encouragement, they had grown equally strong. Though they might have preferred to serve together the rest of their lives, God had a more practical plan. He had other young preachers He wanted each man to train. As a result of their differing convictions, two preachers became four, and soon we'll see another. Paul and Barnabas went their separate ways—two mentors, each with a new apprentice. The empty place in Paul's ministry left an appropriate space for a man named Silas to fill.

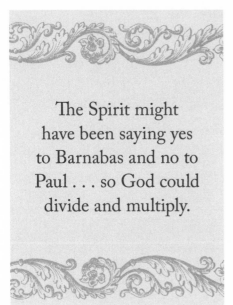

Scripture tells us most divisions are not of God, but Acts 15 suggests that sometimes God wants to divide and multiply. Can you imagine how much simpler church life could be if we accepted that God could place two people under different convictions to multiply ministry? I've seen this phenomenon occur at my own church. Two very strong leaders in our church differed over whether we should have traditional worship or contemporary worship. Who was right? Both of them. God divided one worship service into two, and we now reach more people.

Often differences erupt due to less noble motivations—two opinionated people unwilling to budge. And unless we invite God to come to the rescue, the results can be disastrous. Ministries and partnerships often divide and dwindle rather than divide and multiply. On the other hand, when God leads two people who have walked together to a fork in the road, He can do something wonderful—*if* they and their constituents are mature enough to deal with it!

How do you go about determining the Lord's will when a faithful brother or sister (or spouse or relative) is sure that another way is best? ______________________________

____

____

____

____

____

____

PRAYING GOD'S WORD TODAY

Lord, You have warned us not to argue about doubtful issues (Rom. 14:1), to diligently keep the unity of the Spirit with the peace that binds us (Eph. 4:3). Help us, then, not to judge anything prematurely, before the Lord comes, for You will bring to light what is hidden in darkness and reveal the intentions of the hearts. And then praise will come to each of us from You (1 Cor. 4:5) as we follow You, submit to You, and faithfully seek to honor You.

Day 27

When Christians Clash

BEFORE YOU BEGIN

Read Acts 15:39–41

STOP AND CONSIDER

There was such a sharp disagreement that they parted company,
and Barnabas took Mark with him and sailed off to Cyprus. (v. 39)

What is a current or recent difference of opinion you've had with your church leadership or with another believer over spiritual or ministry matters? How are you handling it?

How have you seen these types of disagreements take on a life of their own, spinning far out of control? What usually feeds and fuels this kind of result?

Day 28

Lessons from a Friend

Before You Begin

Read Acts 16:1–3

Stop and Consider

He went on to Derbe and Lystra, where there was a disciple named Timothy, the son of a believing Jewish woman, but his father was a Greek. (v. 1)

Think of one of your dearest friends. What are the unique qualities you most appreciate about this person? What have you learned about yourself through this rare relationship?

What elements of your life and your past—things you have often deemed to be a negative or drawback—could God use to make you more effective in ministry, even to make you a better friend?

One of my favorite parts of studying Paul's life is exploring some of his friendships; yet as many as he had, one would differ from all the rest. Many years later I'm sure his heart was washed with emotion as he recalled his return to Lystra and the risk he took on a young man named Timothy. From the very beginning, Timothy was special. Allow Scripture to shed some light on his distinctives.

1. *Timothy was a unique choice because of his youthfulness.* In 1 Timothy 4:12, Paul counseled Timothy not to let anyone look down on him because of his youth, yet even this piece of advice came a full fifteen years after Timothy had joined Paul. Paul's words in 2 Timothy 3:15 demonstrate that in spite of his youth, Timothy was fertile soil from which ministry grew: "From childhood you have known the sacred Scriptures, which are able to instruct you for salvation through faith in Christ Jesus." I believe Paul saw Timothy's tremendous potential for fruit bearing. The opportunity to train him while he was still young and teachable was probably a benefit to Paul's ministry, not a hindrance.

Do you know any young people who are trying to be genuine servants of God? If so, they may be discouraged because no one is taking them seriously. Why not make a point of encouraging a young servant through a note, a call, or a pat on the back?

2. *Timothy had a unique upbringing.* He came from a family with a Jewish mother and a Greek father. You may have an insight into Timothy's childhood because of differences in your own parents' belief systems. Growing up in a home with one believing and one unbelieving parent is hard. In those days, having a Jewish mother who had accepted Christ and a Greek father who didn't believe would have been both difficult and different.

My generation was the first to be raised on films and fairy tales in living color. Movies like *Cinderella*, *Snow White*, and *Beauty and the Beast* redefine romance as two people from different worlds falling deeply in love. Typically their only problem is their unyielding family. Love ultimately overcomes and they live happily ever after. We need to teach our children the truth about real romance and love that lasts. The sparks that fly from two different worlds converging in one couple usually end up burning someone!

Paul delivered a strong exhortation in 2 Corinthians 6:14 (NIV): "Do not be yoked together with unbelievers." The Greek word for "yoked" is *zugos*, which means "a yoke serving to couple any two things together and a coupling, a beam of a balance which unites two scales, hence a balance." In the next verse Paul asked a question to make his point: "What harmony is there?" When two completely different belief systems are joined together, the result often is a lack of balance and harmony.

God wasted nothing in either Paul's or Timothy's background. He won't waste anything in yours either.

You may have grown up in this kind of home, so you know how rocky this life can be. Perhaps you may presently be in a home where spiritual beliefs differ drastically. If so, I hope you receive some encouragement from Timothy's experience. God can prevail and bear wonderful fruit from an unequally yoked couple as we will see, even though their lives are often more complicated than they had to be.

3. *Timothy had a unique perspective.* He had been intimately exposed to three practices he and Paul would encounter in ministry: agnosticism because of his father's unbelief, Judaism because of his mother's heritage, and Christianity because of his mother's acceptance of Christ as Messiah and Savior. Even though he did not have the security of two believing parents, he gained an insight that would prove valuable in ministry. God wasted nothing in either Paul's or Timothy's background. He won't waste anything in your background either, if you will allow Him to use you.

4. *Timothy had a unique maturity.* In our society we've almost become convinced that bad influences are stronger than good. Timothy certainly is evidence to the contrary. We have a wonderful biblical precedent proving that godly influence can carry a much heavier weight than ungodly influence.

The words of 2 Timothy 1:5 offer strong encouragement to anyone married to an unbeliever. Paul wrote of the "sincere faith that first lived in your grandmother Lois, then in your mother Eunice, and that I am convinced is in you also." Yes, you can rear godly children in spite of imperfect circumstances. Lois and Eunice lived their faith. Timothy saw genuine examples of faithfulness. Their lives were devoted to God even when the company left. They were genuine—not perfect, but real. Their sincerity won Timothy to the truth.

Hang in there, parent! Let your children see the sincerity of your faith. Let them see you praying and trusting. Nothing carries the weight of sincere faith!

For Christ, Paul sacrificed many things dear to the Jew: marriage, children, strong extended family. God honored Paul's sacrifice by giving him other priceless gifts. Timothy was one of those gifts. He filled a void in Paul's life that no one else ever matched. Years later Paul described Timothy as "my dear son." Perhaps God thought a crusty old preacher needed a young whippersnapper as much as Timothy needed him.

What constitutes your heritage of faith? You may have a Christian heritage from only one side of your family. Or you may be the first believer in several generations. How has God used these blessings (or these obstacles) to reveal His grace and love to you?

Praying God's Word Today

Lord, Your solemn Word declares that You are a jealous God, punishing the children for the fathers' sin to the third and fourth generations (Exod. 20:5). Yet more glorious and powerful is the fact that You are the faithful God who keeps Your gracious covenant loyalty for a thousand generations with those who love You and keep Your commands (Deut. 7:9). Thank You, my Father, that sin and rebellion are not the only heritage passed down to future generations—that faithfulness has an even greater influence!

Day 29

Change of Plans

Before You Begin

Read Acts 16:4–8

Stop and Consider

When they came to Mysia, they tried to go into Bithynia, but the Spirit of Jesus did not allow them. So, bypassing Mysia, they came down to Troas. (vv. 7–8)

Have you ever experienced this kind of resistance from the Spirit to a particular course of action or decision? What was the result of your acceptance (or rejection) of His counsel?

With so many possible reasons for feeling led a certain way, how do you sort out the Holy Spirit's voice from all others? How would you advise someone to navigate this?

Romans 8:9 tells us God has placed His Spirit within each person who has received Christ. One reason His Spirit takes up residence inside us is to tell us things only believers can understand, leading us in areas of obedience to Christ. The Holy Spirit always leads believers in Christ, but we don't always recognize His leadership. A few basic practices can help us follow the leadership of the Holy Spirit.

1. *Study God's Word.* God will never lead us in any direction contrary to His Word.

2. *Yield to the Holy Spirit's control.* Being yielded to God's authority keeps us pliable and open-minded to a possible change of plans.

3. *Pray for clear leadership.* Adopt David's approach to prayer in Psalm 27:11, asking God to teach you His ways and lead you in a straight path.

4. *Pray for wisdom and discernment to recognize specific directions.* Paul asked God to give believers "a spirit of wisdom and revelation" (Eph. 1:17) to know Him better. This request is a good guideline for us too.

5. *Make plans, but hold on to them loosely!* I don't believe God intended for Paul, Silas, and Timothy to travel haphazardly through the countryside. Paul was a very intelligent man. He probably formulated an itinerary just like most of us would, but he kept his plans open just in case God had different ideas!

6. *Learn to recognize peace as one of God's prompters.* Peace is one of the most obvious earmarks of the authority of Christ. A sense of peace will virtually always accompany His will and direction—even when the direction might not have been our personal preference. On the other hand, a lack of peace will often accompany a mistaken path—even when the direction is definitely our personal preference. Remember, Christ is the Prince of Peace. His peace will accompany His authority.

More than any other disciple, Paul was used of God to teach about the activity of the Holy Spirit. But Paul could not teach what he had never learned. He learned to follow the leadership of the Holy Spirit one day at a time, one city at a time. Let's learn from his example and be willing to change our course when we sense God has different plans.

Praying God's Word Today

Lord, You have taught us in Your Word that no wisdom, no understanding, and no counsel will prevail against You (Prov. 21:30). May I never be guilty of choosing my personal preferences and inclinations over Your clear guidance. And when I am unsure about Your specific directions, may I be willing to wait for You, knowing that You give us our food at the right time. And when You give it to us, we gather it; when You open Your hand, we are satisfied with good things (Ps. 104:27–28).

Day 30

Lydia's Legacy

Before You Begin

Read Acts 16:9–15

Stop and Consider

Lydia, a dealer in purple cloth from the city of Thyatira, who worshiped God, was listening. The Lord opened her heart to pay attention to what was spoken by Paul. (v. 14)

Do you deal with inferiority very often, convinced you're not as talented or important as others are? If so, how has this affected your life? How has it minimized your influence?

To see God dramatically direct Paul and his companions from the mission fields of Asia to the house of Lydia should encourage us. What do you make of His singular love for you?

Paul and his small band of missionaries did not have to wait long for redirection after God removed their sense of peace and approval, prompting them not to enter the province of Asia. Following their willingness to allow God to change their plans, He used a vision to lead them into uncharted territory—a vision of a man from Macedonia begging Paul, "Cross over to Macedonia and help us!" (Acts 16:9). As a result, the missionary band traveled to Philippi where Paul found no synagogue, so he preached at a gathering place outside the city.

There by the river he encountered a woman named Lydia. We've seen Paul have more thrilling encounters. Nothing outwardly dramatic happened. Almost seemed ho-hum, didn't it? Was this all that God had in mind—one woman's reception of the gospel—when He resisted their plans to preach His Word in the direction they were headed? But after temporarily closing a door in the province of Asia, God strained their eyes to see a much wider vision. The gospel of Jesus Christ went to Europe! Within a couple hundred years, Christians numbered in the tens of thousands in Europe. We hear people say, "When God closes a door, He opens a window." Sometimes we might just be underestimating Him. We just saw Him close a door and open a continent.

And it all started with a businesswoman named Lydia.

No one would ever suspect some of the feelings of spiritual inferiority professional Christian businesswomen harbor at times. For everyone who ever wondered if God could use a professional businesswoman, meet Lydia. She was a city girl, a salesperson. A homeowner with enough room to house a host of people. Yet her professional life was balanced by the priorities of her spiritual life. She worshipped God. She didn't see the Sabbath as an opportunity to catch up on some sleep and straighten up the house. She gathered with other believers. She found a place of prayer (v. 13). She opened her home. She made herself available to God. Because she did, "the Lord opened her heart" to hear Paul's message. And God gave birth to the gospel in Europe. I'd say that businesswoman had a pretty important ministry, wouldn't you?

Praying God's Word Today

O Lord, how I long to be like those five faithful women who, when the bridegroom arrived and the others were out buying oil for their lamps, were ready to go in with him—with You—to the wedding banquet (Matt. 25:10). Keep me assured of Your faithful love and anticipating Your forever presence.

Day 31

Watching in Horror

Before You Begin

Read Acts 16:16–24

Stop and Consider

They said, "These men are seriously disturbing our city. They are Jews, and are promoting customs that are not legal for us as Romans to adopt or practice." (vv. 20–21)

What are the differences between going through a painful ordeal yourself and watching another endure a similarly difficult trial? Which is harder, do you think, and why?

Even today, many are being actively persecuted for their faith. How often does their plight come to mind? How can you make your prayer for them more deliberate and diligent?

You may be wondering why four men preached the gospel in Philippi but only two of them were punished. Where were Luke and Timothy when the sparks started flying? The Roman world had recently experienced a fresh surge of anti-Semitism, and Emperor Claudius had expelled all Jews from Rome. Because few things are more contagious than prejudice, Philippi (a Roman colony) quickly caught the virus. Timothy and Luke may have been considered Gentiles by the Roman authorities. Since the governors of Philippi knew virtually nothing about Christianity, Paul and Silas were dragged before a strongly anti-Semitic magistrate and persecuted because of their Jewish heritage.

Imagine how the foursome felt: divided over their backgrounds, two were freed, and two were carried away maliciously. I'm not at all sure which two had the easier sentence. The book of Hebrews acknowledges the kinds of roles both pairs played: "Remember the earlier days when, after you had been enlightened, you endured a hard struggle with sufferings. Sometimes you were publicly exposed to taunts and afflictions, and at other times you were companions of those who were treated that way (Heb. 10:32–33).

God is very aware that standing close to someone who is hurting hurts! He does it every day. But whether we are the ones suffering or we're alongside another, His grace is sufficient for our need. So you can cry out for help, even when you're hurting for someone else. He'll hear you and acknowledge your need!

Luke and Timothy deeply needed God's comfort as they watched the severe flogging of their partners. First, Paul and Silas were stripped—an incomprehensible humiliation to anyone with a Jewish background. Then they were mercilessly beaten with rods.

Paul probably suffered in both ways. He suffered his own blows, but he also stood by Silas as he was stripped and severely whipped. Can you imagine how Paul ached for his new assistant? Did he wonder if Silas could take it? If so, he found that no one needed to underestimate Silas. Luke and Timothy strained for a last look at their partners as the authorities dragged them to prison, wondering if they would ever see them again. In some ways, Luke and Timothy's night may have been longer than Silas and Paul's.

Praying God's Word Today

Lord God, we know it has been given to us on Christ's behalf not only to believe in You, but also to suffer for You (Phil. 1:29). But may we, like Paul, be able to say, "After we had previously suffered and been outrageously treated in Philippi, as you know, we were emboldened by our God to speak the gospel of God to you in spite of great opposition" (1 Thess. 2:2). May dark days draw me ever closer to You, being strengthened for greater service to You and others as You work through my weakened body and humble spirit.

Day 32

Midnight Song

Before You Begin

Read Acts 16:25–34

Stop and Consider

About midnight Paul and Silas were praying and singing hymns to God, and the prisoners were listening to them. (v. 25)

Why does music uniquely draw us into a mind-set of worship, thanks, and perspective? What would our world be like without the outlet of singing and rejoicing?

Can you describe a time when God pushed forth a song from your lips, when singing was the last thing that made sense at the moment?

The two bloodied servants of God—Paul and Silas—had been taken to a dungeon and placed in stocks, unable to move, pain wracking their bodies. Yet though they were bound in iron chains, they found freedom to sing.

We cheat the faithful servants from showing us God's glory if we believe God chose to anesthetize their pain. The awful truth is that death would have been a relief. The challenge of their moment was living until the pain became bearable—pain that is never more vivid than in the midnight hour. The night lacks the kindness of the day when demands and activities distract. Each time their hearts beat, every nerve ending throbbed with pain. In spite of their anguish, their prayers ascended before the throne, and God gave them "songs in the night" (Job 35:10).

Prayers come naturally when we are distressed—but songs? Finding notes is difficult when your body is gripped with pain. Nonetheless, these few notes found their way into a melody, and their melodies turned into hymns. Every stanza issued a fresh strength and their voices were unchained—penetrating walls and bars.

The most difficult part of my service as a Sunday school teacher has been watching my members bury loved ones. Several years ago one of my members lost her fifteen-year-old son in an automobile accident. I will never forget accompanying our friend to the funeral home and helping her choose a casket. All four of us walked to the car and drove away without saying a word. Within a couple of blocks, one of us began to cry, and then the rest joined her without saying a word. Then after several minutes of silence, another began to sing with broken notes, "I love you, Lord . . . and I lift my voice . . . to worship You . . . O, my soul rejoice." I could hardly believe the nerve of my fellow member to sing at a time like that. But before I could look at her with proper horror, the mother's best friend joined in, "Take joy, my King, in what You hear . . . may it be a sweet, sweet sound in Your ear."

The words fell from their lips a second time and to my shock, the brokenhearted mother began to sing. If *she* could sing, I knew I could not remain silent. So we sang the rest of the way home that day. Not one of us had a solo voice, and yet I wonder if I will ever hear a sound so beautiful again. I knew then what God meant when He told us to lift up the sacrifice of praise. When praise is the last thing that comes naturally to us and we choose to worship Him anyway, we've had the privilege of offering a genuine sacrifice of praise.

> The message is never more clear than when God's people refuse to cease their praises during intense suffering.

When we sing a midnight song or speak praises in the darkest hours, the chains of hopelessness not only drop from our ankles but sometimes from the ankles of those who listen. We can preach the gospel in many ways, but the message is never more clear than when God's people refuse to cease their praises during intense suffering.

In their bondage, Paul and Silas were free to sing. They were also free to stay. Finally their songs were eclipsed by the rumblings of an earthquake. The foundations of the prison trembled before an awesome God. The prison doors flew open, every chain was loosed, and the jailer drew his sword to kill himself. Paul's words to him penetrate my heart: "Don't harm yourself!" (Acts 16:28). How many people have felt compelled to harm themselves over hopelessness? The jailer knew he would be held responsible for their escape. "Don't harm yourself, because all of us are here!" shouted Paul.

Sometimes God frees us from chains so we can turn our backs on our slavery and walk away like Peter in Acts 12. He was free to leave. As a result, the church that was praying for his release was edified. Other times God frees us from chains so we can remain where we are to share the message of freedom with other captives. Paul was free to stay, not to leave. Because he did, a man asked, "'What must I do to be saved?'" (16:30). And an entire household found sweet liberty.

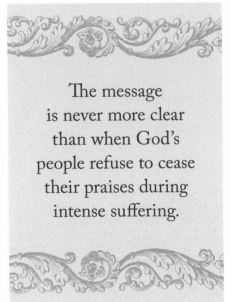

I met a young man who had experienced freedom from the bondage of homosexuality. Although he was a dedicated servant, God had never appointed him to share that part of his testimony nor minister to those still chained in that lifestyle. Like Peter, he had been freed to leave. Yet after God delivered me from the bondage of my childhood victimization, He called me to share my basic testimony and reach out to other survivors of abuse. I had been freed to stay. Both my friend and I experienced the glorious freedom of Christ. One was free to leave and one was free to stay, but we each trust God with His perfect plan for our lives.

God reserves the right to use His servants and their experiences in different ways. Let's try to resist copying a blueprint from another person's ministry. God is very creative, and He always has purpose in the specific ways He chooses to use us. Be willing to allow Him to put some things to public use and other things to private use. As life draws us to extremes, may we pass our tests as Paul and Silas did—with a song.

Called to leave. Called to stay. Which of these best describes your calling in regard to your life history? Have you perhaps mistakenly chosen one over the other, and you're suffering the unrest and new scars to show for it? Spend some time thinking about this.

Praying God's Word Today

Deep calls to deep, Lord, in the roar of Your waterfalls; all Your breakers and Your billows have swept over me. You will send Your faithful love by day; Your song will be with me in the night—a prayer to the God of my life (Ps. 42:7–8). I cling to this hope, and pray for a song.

Day 33

Getting with the Program

Before You Begin

Read Acts 17:1–9

Stop and Consider

As usual, Paul went to them, and on three Sabbath days
reasoned with them from the Scriptures. (v. 2)

Some people think that being spiritual means living by the seat of our pants, just going with the flow. But Paul seemed to operate with some patterns. What does that tell you?

Where do you fall on the flexibility spectrum? Are you more charts and calendars, or more whims and whatevers? And how do the two of us go together in God's body?

Our next passage takes us to another stop on Paul's second missionary journey—the Greek city of Thessalonica. We know Luke had accompanied the missionaries to Philippi, but his terminology suggests that their paths parted for awhile, presumably for the sake of the gospel. Luke's references to "we" rather than "they" will pick up again several chapters later in the book of Acts. For now we see Paul and Silas in Thessalonica.

Before we proceed, let's highlight a few points from this passage at the beginning of Acts 17. Paul and Silas had traveled one hundred miles from Philippi to Thessalonica without the benefit of a motorized vehicle. They seemed to know exactly where they wanted to go and certainly did not lack the stamina to get there!

You may be wondering what criteria made one city more of a priority than another. Obviously the first criteria was the leadership of the Holy Spirit. If He did not lead, they did not go. Paul cited another criteria in Romans 15:20, when he declared, "My aim is to evangelize where Christ has not been named, in order that I will not be building on someone else's foundation."

God used both of these principles: the leadership of the Holy Spirit and Paul's desire to go into territories untouched by the gospel. And in each new venue, not only did Paul customarily preach in the synagogues first, he employed the same method each time. He sought to prove that Jesus was the Christ with the Old Testament Scripture. I believe he used this method with them because God had used it so effectively on him in the desert of Arabia. He knew this technique could work on the hardest of hearts because it had worked so well on his.

As a result, some Jews and many Greeks believed. But wherever there is an awakening, you can always expect opposition. It wasn't long before the seed of jealousy was planted in other Jews. They incited a riot, storming the house of Jason, Paul's host in Thessalonica, searching in vain for a crack at "these men who have turned the world upside down" (v. 6). We see method. We see message. We see patterns and expectations. We see a man serving God with a perfect blend of spiritual sensitivity and dogged determination.

Praying God's Word Today

Lord, Your Word teaches us to finalize plans through counsel, to wage war with sound guidance (Prov. 20:18), that the plans of the diligent certainly lead to profit, but anyone who is reckless only becomes poor (Prov. 21:5). But because there are many plans in a man's heart, and only Your decree will prevail (Prov. 19:21), I pray that You would align my thoughts with Yours so that I can walk in Your way.

Day 34

By the Book

Before You Begin

Read Acts 17:10–14

Stop and Consider

They welcomed the message with eagerness and examined the Scriptures daily to see if these things were so. (v. 11)

What are some of your most effective ways of digesting the Word? What have you found to be the best ways to keep it alive in your heart and fresh on your mind?

What are some qualities about the Scriptures you only notice when you're actively engaged with them consistently over a long period of time?

The Christians in Thessalonica got Paul out of jail and sent him to Berea. Only twenty miles from the sea, Berea had everything to offer: warm coastal breezes tempered by snow-capped mountains. What could be more inviting than a city set between the mountains and the ocean? Exceeding the noble sight, however, was the nobility of the people. The Bereans possessed characteristics that provide an excellent standard for believers today:

1. *They were willing to receive.* Acts 17:11 tells us the Bereans received the message. The Greek word for "receive" is *dechomai*, which means "to accept an offer deliberately and readily." The Bereans accepted the offer to come and hear what Paul had to say.

Many churches work overtime to offer opportunities for Christian growth and encouragement: conferences, retreats, Bible studies, discipleship training, and other methods. Often a relative few attend. And sometimes the ones who don't are the very ones who criticize the church for not doing enough. Many times we don't lack opportunities; we lack willingness. The Bereans accepted the offer to hear Paul teach and preach, and the fruit was bountiful.

2. *They were ready to receive.* The Bereans not only accepted the offer to hear Paul; they were eager to receive what he said. The original word for "eagerness" is *prothumia*, which indicates a predisposition for learning (Strong's). Our experiences in Bible study, worship services, and other discipleship opportunities are greatly enhanced when we approach each one with a predisposition for learning. We need to prepare ourselves with everything we can to have a receptive disposition before we arrive.

3. *They cross-examined the message with the Scriptures.* Paul was a very effective communicator, yet the Bereans did not take his word for everything. They measured the accuracy of his message against Scripture through their own personal examination of the Word. The original word for "examined" in Acts 17:11 is *anakrino*, which means "to ask, question, discern, examine, judge, search" (Strong's).

We all need to learn to study the Scriptures for ourselves. All believers have the right to ask questions and examine the Scriptures to check the accuracy of the teaching they hear. Congregations can be easily misled if they do not feel or exercise the freedom to double-check teaching and preaching against the Word of God. A savvy communicator can use the Scriptures taken out of context to teach almost anything! Any portion of Scripture must be compared with Scripture as a whole.

> We can grow so accustomed to being spoon-fed the Word of God that we forget how to examine it for ourselves.

Some years ago a national forest had to close off a portion of its park to tourists. A number of bears starved to death during the time the park was closed. They had grown so accustomed to being fed by the tourists, they had ceased feeding themselves. We can likewise grow so accustomed to being spoon-fed the Word of God that we forget how to examine the Scriptures for ourselves. We can cease checking the nutritional value of what we're being taught!

But the Bereans not only performed the right practices, I believe they possessed the right heart. They didn't examine the Scriptures to see if they could find error in how Paul had dotted an "i" or crossed a "t." Their motive was not to argue. Some people double-check their pastors and teachers on every issue just to find an error so they can feel superior. The Bereans had no such motive. So a wonderful and sometimes rare combination occurred in Berea: the best kind of preacher met the best kind of audience. And a great awakening of faith resulted.

But soon the Jews in Thessalonica found out Paul was preaching in Berea and were vindictive enough to travel fifty miles to agitate and stir up the people! The original word for "stir up" has an interesting meaning. *Saleuo* means "to rock, topple, shake, stir up" (Strong's). The enemy of our souls will use every means and every human agent he can to topple us. And if all we have going for us are the opinions of men through sermons or lessons, little will be left when life shakes us up. But when we've learned to examine the Scriptures for ourselves, we have a few things nailed down when life starts to rock.

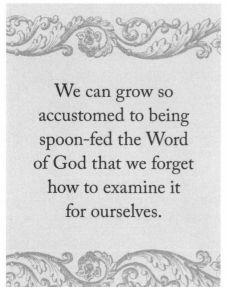

As you continue to study the Word of God, one nailed-down, personally discovered truth will turn into many, and you will be better equipped to face anything that comes your way. Nothing will profit you more than learning to examine the Scriptures for yourself. Let every preacher and teacher be a catalyst to your own personal journey through the Word. Spend time exploring. Invest in an exhaustive Bible concordance, a good Bible dictionary, and a sound set of commentaries. Accept opportunities to get into in-depth Bible studies and really get to know the Word. Be ready and willing to receive from the many opportunities available, but with the ability to discern truth from error through deep personal examinations of the Scripture. Imitating the noble practices of the Bereans will be your safety as teachers come and go—and your sanity when life rocks and rolls.

How has the Word balanced you during times of spiritual shaking and quaking? How has it kept you from falling apart when everything seemed to be falling apart around you?

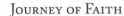

Praying God's Word Today

Lord God, Your decrees are wonderful; therefore I obey them. The revelation of Your words brings light and gives understanding to the inexperienced. I pant with open mouth because I long for Your commands. Turn to me and be gracious to me, as is Your practice toward those who love Your name (Ps. 119:129–132).

Day 35

Variation on a Theme

Before You Begin

Read Acts 17:15–23

Stop and Consider

I even found an altar on which was inscribed: TO AN UNKNOWN GOD. Therefore, what you worship in ignorance, this I proclaim to you. (v. 23)

What keeps you the most distracted and unaware of openings for spiritual conversation with others? What could keep you more tuned in to these opportunities?

Just sitting here, far from the heat of the moment, what are some of the current, cultural analogies you could use to get people talking about their need for God?

Come along as we see a lesson in contrasts. The next audience Paul encountered differed drastically from the noble Bereans. Meet the ancient Athenians. They will make you wonder how people who knew so much could understand so little.

Paul had a fruitful ministry at Berea until troublemakers came from Thessalonica. Then at the urging of the believers, Paul once again found himself moving on. This time the destination was Athens. Some of the believers escorted Paul there and left him, where he awaited the arrival of Silas and Timothy.

So Paul had to encounter the imposing city of Athens all by himself. And according to Acts 17:16, he reacted strongly to the sight of a city full of idols. Imagine going on a mission trip to a city like Varanasi, India—a Hindu holy city filled with temples and images depicting hundreds of gods. Yet here we have a tender opportunity to see the sincerity of Paul's heart, for "he reasoned in the synagogue with the Jews and with those who worshiped God, and in the marketplace every day with those who happened to be there" (v. 17). He had no emotional or spiritual support and probably little physical support. None of the others would have known if he had simply been too intimidated to preach. No one would have blamed him anyway. Yet day by day he tried to reason with any Athenian who would listen, because he was so concerned that they needed Jesus Christ.

This audience of philosophers lived to hear some new idea and invited Paul to their meeting of the Areopagus on Mars Hill. There he preached an unusual sermon. He reached across the gulf of culture and beliefs that separated his hearers from Christ, finding an object lesson from their culture that he used to share the gospel with them. He found that they had an altar with this inscription: "to an unknown god." Beginning from that point, Paul shared the gospel with the philosophers. He said in effect, "Let me tell you about this God you don't know."

I believe Acts 17 contains one of the best sermons he ever preached. He used the perfect illustration (the unknown God) and drew his audience to the perfect invitation.

Praying God's Word Today

I pray, Lord, that You will continually open a door to us for the message, to speak the mystery of Christ. May we always walk in wisdom toward outsiders, making the most of the time—our speech gracious, seasoned with salt, so that we may know how we should answer each person (Col. 4:3–6).

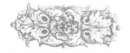

Day 36

Who Cares?

Before You Begin

Read Acts 17:24–34

Stop and Consider

Some began to ridicule him. But others said, "We will hear you about this again." So Paul went out from their presence. (vv. 32–33)

Which do you find more difficult to deal with: opposition or apathy? In what ways have you experienced both? ____

____

____

Where apathy exists, what has usually occurred to bring it about? How do we best guard ourselves against letting it characterize us? ____

____

____

____

Paul never mentions a church resulting from his work in Athens. Only a few people became believers there, and he never made contact with them again as far as we know. Based on the information in Scripture, the few believers never multiplied into more.

And yet notice that he was not persecuted in Athens, nor was he forced to leave the city. Acts 18:1 tells us he simply left. Glance back over the previous chapters of the book of Acts. Compare this trip to the many others in Paul's ministry. Count the times he ran into very little opposition or persecution. You will search in vain to find another experience exactly like the one he had in Athens.

Why didn't they lift a hand to persecute him? Because they were too cold to care. Paul's experience in Athens is a perfect example of a situation in which people were open-minded to a fault. Their motto was "anything goes." Everyone was welcome to his own philosophy. Live and let live! If it works for you, go for it! Athens was the birthplace of the tolerance movement.

Often persecution is not nearly the enemy that indifference is. The Athenians did not care if Paul stayed or left. They believed virtually everyone was entitled to his god. A few sneered. Others were polite enough to say they would be willing to listen to his strange teachings again. But most never realized Paul was escorted into town by the one true God. And most never cared.

Acts 17 has changed the way I pray about the nations. I cannot count the times I've asked God to crumble the spirit of opposition and persecution in many nations where Christians are a small fighting force. I will still continue to ask God to strengthen and protect those facing opposition and persecution. However, I now find my heart drawn across the map to places where a quieter dragon of perhaps equal force has made its den—the spirit of indifference. Christianity can grow and flourish under some of the most difficult opposition, but it will prosper very little where people refuse to be changed by it. Paul's experience in Athens proves that the best of sermons will never change an unwilling person's heart.

PRAYING GOD'S WORD TODAY

Lord, You have commanded that Your precepts be diligently kept (Ps. 119:4). Therefore, may we constantly be on our guard and diligently watch ourselves, so that we don't forget the things our eyes have seen or let them slip from our minds as long as we live. May we also be faithful to teach Your Word to our children and grandchildren (Deut. 4:9), encouraging them never to grow tired of doing good, for we will reap at the proper time if we don't give up (Gal. 6:9).

Day 37

Failure to Communicate

Before You Begin

Read 1 Corinthians 2:1–5

Stop and Consider

When I came to you, brothers, announcing the testimony of God to you,
I did not come with brilliance of speech or wisdom. (v. 1)

Why would God think it appropriate to report on events when someone like Paul was having a bad day, when he was revealing his marked lack of resemblance to Superman?

What are your typical follow-up feelings after an episode of perceived failure or after an embarrassing situation? What usually happens next? Who and what do you avoid?

I suspect that Paul's visit to Athens affected him far more than we realize. Few people believed and received Christ. Paul was overwhelmed by the polytheistic beliefs of the residents. They wanted to argue philosophies rather than consider the truth. The Athenians did not throw Paul out of the city or persecute him in any obvious way. The few converts appear to have produced little fruit. Apparently no church was established. Paul spent most of his days in Athens alone. Although 1 Thessalonians 3:1 indicates Timothy and Silas might have come as he asked, they were quickly sent elsewhere. After a brief stay in Athens, he simply moved on in frustration.

Paul had plenty of time to think on his way to Corinth. He spent several grueling days alone. During those long hours, I believe he convinced himself that every effort in Athens had failed. As we often do, I suspect he became so focused on the negative that he lost sight of the positive.

Have you ever noticed how lengthy times of solitude affect us differently depending on our state of mind? Aloneness exaggerates our emotions and sensitivities. For example, we can sometimes sense the presence of God and hear His voice far more clearly when we have several days alone. But on the other hand, solitude can also exaggerate negative feelings. We find ourselves almost thinking too much! We look back on a situation and decide nothing good came from it at all. Insecurity turns into immobilization, and intimidation turns into terror! If you have ever had a lengthy time alone in which your mind "ran away with you" on the wings of negative thoughts, then you probably understand something of what Paul was feeling.

I believe the more Paul thought about his experiences in Athens, the worse he felt. First Corinthians 2:1 may suggest that Paul felt intimidated by the Athenians, and these feelings accompanied him to Corinth. Athens attracted intellectuals who could debate eloquently and were eager to flaunt their knowledge. As he tried to preach to them, the Epicurean and Stoic philosophers disputed with him. Some sneered, "What is this pseudo-intellectual trying to say?" (Acts 17:18).

Paul had been the pride of his graduating class—the child prodigy! You can imagine the beating his ego took in Athens. I think Paul felt like a failure. First Corinthians 2:2 says by the time he reached Corinth, he had "determined to know nothing . . . except Jesus Christ and Him crucified." Thank goodness, he knew the only thing he really had to know! He determined to base his life and ministry on Christ—his one certainty!

> Paul knew the only thing he really had to know. He determined to base his life and ministry on Christ, his one certainty!

In 1 Corinthians we see an insight Paul eventually gained from his experience. Are these words evidence that he may have been thinking back on the Athenians? "For to those who are perishing the message of the cross is foolishness, but to us who are being saved it is God's power. For it is written: 'I will destroy the wisdom of the wise, and I will set aside the understanding of the experts'" (1 Cor. 1:18–19).

God used this entire experience to show Paul an important lesson. In 1 Corinthians 2:14 he wrote, "But the natural man does not welcome what comes from God's Spirit, because it is foolishness to him; he is not able to know it since it is evaluated spiritually." Paul ultimately gained the insights he wrote about in 1 Corinthians, but as he traveled to Corinth he was still in turmoil. On the miles between Athens and Corinth, Paul probably hashed and rehashed his experiences. He wished he had said this or that. Sometimes we can't explain exactly what we believe. Other times we think of just the right answer when it's too late. We end up feeling foolish because we weren't persuasive.

Obviously Paul's experience had a great impact on his next opportunity. He entered Corinth "in weakness, in fear, and in much trembling" (1 Cor. 2:3). The word "weakness" comes from an original word used for a sickness. It suggests that Paul was so scared he was physically ill. The word for "trembling" indicates something we've all experienced: hands shaking from nervousness. The opposite word is "confidence." By the time Paul reached

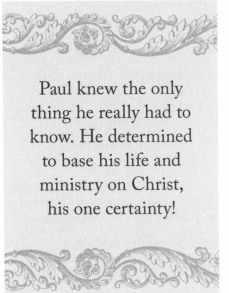

Corinth, he had lost his confidence. Possibly he wondered if the fruit he had seen in other cities had come from God's blessings on Barnabas or Silas.

Does seeing Paul's experience in this light help you to relate to him as a fellow struggler on the road to serve Christ? You probably didn't know the apostle Paul shared the same feelings. Neither did I. I hope you can find encouragement in his experience.

The enemy would have enjoyed preventing Paul from ministering in Corinth because of feelings of inadequacy, but Satan was unsuccessful. God instead used Paul's feelings to give a great "demonstration of the Spirit and power" (1 Cor. 2:4). The word for "demonstration" in this passage is *apodeixis*, meaning "proof." What a wonderful term! Do you see what Paul meant? He was so intimidated by the time he reached Corinth, the abundant fruit ultimately produced through his preaching was proof of the Holy Spirit's power! God sometimes uses us most powerfully when we feel the least adequate.

When was the last time you lost your confidence? When did you last have to do something that made you so nervous your hands shook and you were physically ill? What did you learn about yourself (and about God) in the process? ______

Praying God's Word Today

Father, when we are struggling and unsure of ourselves, you say to us: "Strengthen the weak hands, steady the shaking knees!" You say to the faint-hearted: "Be strong; do not fear! Here is your God; vengeance is coming. God's retribution is coming; He will save you" (Isa. 35:3–4). I put my trust in Your all-sufficiency today, for You Yourself have said, "I will never leave you or forsake you" (Heb. 13:5).

Day 38

Not Me

BEFORE YOU BEGIN

Read 1 Corinthians 1:26–31

STOP AND CONSIDER

God has chosen the world's foolish things to shame the wise,
and God has chosen the world's weak things to shame the strong. (v. 27)

Do you struggle at times with feelings of inferiority? How do you handle these moments when you feel so inadequate, as if God has surely chosen the wrong person for this?

What are the usual excuses you rationalize in your mind for backing out of responsibility? What lengths do you go to in order to declare yourself unprepared and unworthy?

God often proves Himself when we feel we have the least to offer. And in our passage for today, Paul explained why God sometimes uses this method: so we can be clear that the power comes from Him and not from us. He concluded, "The one who boasts must boast in the Lord." Perhaps Paul's words mean more to you now that you know how he felt when he left Athens.

Just before the taping of my first video series, God allowed me to go through a very difficult time. My confidence took a severe beating. I was so emotionally exhausted that I did not know how I would get through the taping. I sat before the Lord very early the morning we were to begin, and I told Him I did not think I was going to make it. I had worked so hard in preparation; yet as the time arrived, I had nothing to offer.

Thousands of dollars worth of equipment had been shipped to Houston. An amazing number of personnel had worked to prepare. Six cameras had been set in place. An audience had gathered. Everything and everyone was ready—but me. I walked out on that set with only enough strength to get on my knees and pray. But when I got up off my knees to teach, a stream of strength seemed to pour from heaven. Not in buckets. It was more like an intravenous drip. Just enough for me to know He was sustaining me minute by minute. I never felt a rush of adrenaline. I never felt a sudden gust of mighty wind. All I know is that many demanding hours of work took place over the days of that taping, and never did I lack the strength necessary to complete the task. Never in my adult life have I had less confidence, yet He gave me enough of His to keep my knees from buckling.

You may wonder why God allowed me to go through such a difficult season of inadequacy just before that task. I wondered myself until I received the first letter from a viewer of the video series. I wept as I read her words of thanks, and I whispered back, "It was God. Not me." Perhaps God has opened a door for you, but you have no confidence. Is insecurity holding you back from the ministry God has for you? Each of us struggles with insecurities and the loss of confidence. No one has ever been used more mightily than the apostle Paul, yet he was so scared at times he made himself sick!

Praying God's Word Today

Lord God, You have promised to be our confidence and to keep our foot from a snare (Prov. 3:26). You have promised that our strength would be equal to our days, that it would last as long as we live (Deut. 33:25). You said to the apostle Paul, "My grace is sufficient for you, for power is perfected in weakness." Therefore, I will most gladly boast all the more about my weaknesses, so that Your power may reside in me. Because of You, in fact, I am pleased in weaknesses, in insults, in catastrophes, in persecutions, and in pressures. For when I am weak, then I am strong (2 Cor. 12:9–10).

Day 39

Heads Up

Before You Begin

Read Acts 18:12–18

Stop and Consider

Paul, having stayed on for many days, said good-bye to the brothers and sailed away to Syria. . . . He shaved his head at Cenchreae, because he had taken a vow. (v. 18)

We're going to be talking about Paul's reasons for taking this "vow." Do you think vows are an appropriate way of planning or limiting our own behavior? How have you done this?

____

____

How have you seen these kinds of approaches abused in religious life? What are some of the dangers that exist in trying to legislate ourselves? ______________

____

____

____

Dr. Luke seems to have included a sentence of pure trivia in Acts 18; yet in it we may discover a hidden treasure. At first glance, Acts 18:18 seems strange. When Paul left Corinth, he had his hair cut off at Cenchreae because of a vow he had taken.

Luke's writing is so tight, so succinct, his inclusion of Paul's quick stop by the barbershop is almost comical. Why in the world would we need to know Paul got a haircut? Actually, this verse holds a primary key to understanding Paul's visit to Corinth. The point is not the haircut. The point is the reason for Paul's haircut.

Paul's haircut resulted from a vow he had made. Remember, Paul was a Jewish Christian. His Jewish heritage was deeply rooted. He understood that Christ did not save him to make him *forget* his heritage but to *complete* his heritage. At times he still applied some of the former practices of the Jew, not as legalities but as wise choices. Virtually without a doubt, the vow to which Luke was referring was the Nazirite vow.

Numbers 6:1–8 describes the Nazirite vow. The second verse explains the nature and purpose of it: "If a man or woman wants to make a special vow," he or she could employ the Nazarite vow as "a vow of separation to the Lord" (NIV).

The word "wants" identifies the first crucial element of the Nazirite vow—it was strictly voluntary. The word "special" points to the second element. The Nazirite vow was special because of its voluntary nature and because it was offered to men and women alike (v. 2)—unusual in ancient Judaism. Third, notice that the purpose of the Nazirite vow is "separation." The Hebrew word is *pala*, indicating something consecrated to God, distinguished from others, something marvelous and even miraculous often coming from something difficult (Strong's).

Now let's see if we can put this definition into understandable terms. If an Israelite man or woman was going through a time when he or she felt the necessity to be extraordinarily consecrated to God—usually a time of extremely difficult circumstances or temptation—the person would voluntarily take this vow. They knew that in order to be victorious or obedient, they needed extra help and concentration on God.

Paul's recent experiences in Athens were not the only problems he faced in coming to Corinth. He had to confront incredible depravity in this cosmopolitan city. Even by today's standards, Corinth was extremely sexually explicit. The most significant pagan practice was the cult of Aphrodite. Aphrodite represented lust and every kind of sexual perversion. Her followers literally worshipped her through acts of immorality—often in plain sight. Paul had never seen anything remotely like the perversion he would encounter in Corinth.

> We obviously need to avoid temptation, but when we can't help but face it, we can prepare ourselves.

The haircut in verse 18 is not the beginning of the vow. The haircut signaled the end. Before he entered Corinth's gates, Paul wisely committed himself to the vow of the Nazirite so he could maintain consecration to and concentration on Christ, the only One who could lead him to victory (see 2 Cor. 2:14).

Paul's actions teach us an important lesson. We obviously need to avoid temptation, but when we can't help but face it, we can prepare ourselves.

Numbers 6:3 commands anyone taking the Nazirite vow to abstain from wine or strong drink. I have chosen to abstain from alcohol not because I believe alcohol is forbidden, but because I believe it could become a distraction to me. No one told me to abstain from alcohol. I voluntarily made the decision after an honest self-evaluation. I do not believe I could deal with both alcohol and the serious devotion God has asked of me. I can think of too many ways Satan could use it to trap me.

Another practice of the Nazirite provides our clue to understanding the message of Acts 18:18. Those who took the Nazirite vow were to allow their hair to grow long as a physical sign of special devotion to God. That way, if they temporarily forgot their vow, the quickest glance in a mirror would remind them. Also, others would ask why they let their hair grow so long, and this would give them an opportunity to testify about their devotion to God. Once Paul's need for extraordinary consecration to God was over, he went to Cenchreae and got a haircut!

I am impressed with Paul at this point. How about you? His weaknesses, insecurities, and temptations were the same as ours, but he was wise in dealing with them.

Matthew 10:16 is one of my favorite verses. Jesus told His followers to be as "shrewd as serpents and as harmless as doves." Innocence or harmlessness does not mean naïveté. In fact, had Paul approached Corinth naively, he could have gotten into serious trouble. The kind of innocence Christ described was righteousness in spite of reality! That's the kind of righteousness Paul lived. It's the kind we can live as well.

What are some of the particular circumstances or temptations you're enduring right now, challenges that might require you to be more concentrated in your submission to Christ? How could you keep yourself constantly reminded of His presence in your life and of your sold-out devotion to Him? ______________________________

Praying God's Word Today

I call to You, Lord, from the ends of the earth when my heart is without strength. Lead me to a rock that is high above me, for You have been a refuge for me, a strong tower in the face of the enemy. I will live in Your tent forever and take refuge under the shelter of Your wings. For You have heard my vows; You have given a heritage to those who fear You. May I continually sing of Your name, fulfilling my vows day by day (Ps. 61:2–5, 8).

Day 40

Thanks but No Thanks

Before You Begin

Read Acts 18:19–23

Stop and Consider

He himself entered the synagogue and engaged in discussion with the Jews. And though they asked him to stay for a longer time, he declined. (vv. 19–20)

What is your gauge for determining whether a particular ministry opportunity is yours to accomplish or somebody else's? ______________________________

____

____

Thinking of a time when you said yes to something but should have said no, what resulted from your decision to barrel ahead? Did you end up getting burned? How?

____

____

____

When Paul completed his long stay in Corinth, he sailed for Syria, accompanied by a couple he had met and stayed with in Corinth—Priscilla and Aquila. (Their names sound good together, don't they?) Once again the apostle to the Gentiles made a beeline to the synagogue to reason with the Jews, but in Ephesus he found a different reception. The Jews at the synagogue asked him to spend a while with them. This time, however, Paul declined. He went on with his journey to Antioch, leaving Priscilla and Aquila behind.

Do you find Paul's return to the synagogue interesting? Recall his last experience with the Jews in the synagogue of Corinth. He became so frustrated with them, "he shook out his clothes and told them, 'Your blood is on your own heads! I am clean. From now on I will go to the Gentiles'" (Acts 18:6). I thought he had finished preaching to the Jews altogether. But in Ephesus he went right back to the synagogue and reasoned with them again. Paul's ministry was far more productive among the Gentiles, so why did he continue to return to the Jews in virtually every city he visited?

In Romans 9:2–5, Paul answered this question. He so desperately wanted his fellow Jews to know Christ that, if possible, he would have died for them. He could hardly bear for the Jews to miss Christ. He must have been ecstatic over the favorable response of the Jews at the synagogue in Ephesus, but again we see why Paul was such an effective minister and servant. He had surrendered his life to the leadership of the Holy Spirit. He was not driven by his own desires and rationalizations. In his position, I might have convinced myself I was supposed to remain in Ephesus, at least for a while, based on my own desires to see God do a work among a people I loved and an apparent open door. They were begging for more! Yet Acts 18:20 tells us he declined. Paul firmly and lovingly said no.

I have a difficult time saying no. Do you? Paul probably had a difficult time, too, but he was careful to remain focused on God's priorities for him. Paul's example teaches us a timely lesson. The fact that a need exists does not mean God has called me to meet that need. We are wise to trust Him when He seems to be leading us contrary to those things we want to do or those things that seem to be so rational and fitting.

Praying God's Word Today

Lord, Your Word says that people without discernment are doomed (Hos. 4:14)—doomed to making continual mistakes, doomed to finding ourselves separated from Your will and purposes. May I walk so closely to You and in step with Your Spirit that whenever I turn to the right or to the left, my ears will hear this command behind me: "This is the way. Walk in it" (Isa. 30:21). Teach me good judgment and discernment, Lord, for I rely on Your commands (Ps. 119:66).

Day 41

Intramural Competition

BEFORE YOU BEGIN

Read Acts 18:24–28

STOP AND CONSIDER

Being fervent in spirit, he spoke and taught the things about Jesus accurately, although he knew only John's baptism. (v. 25)

What are some of the most glaring (or perhaps subtle) examples of Christian teaching today that delivers much in the way of truth, yet taints it with traces of error?

What makes one preacher or Bible teacher more "popular" than another? And which of these attributes should have little or nothing to do with how accepted their teaching is?

We now get to discover one reason why God did not lead Paul to remain in Ephesus. A Jew named Apollos came there. He was a powerful, passionate preacher with a thorough knowledge of the Scripture. So while Paul may not have known it, his void left an opening for a dazzling preacher. When we can't say no even when God does not give His approval, two unfortunate repercussions often result: we don't do a good job and we don't leave an opening for God's chosen person to fill.

But the account of Apollos gives us one more lesson before we move on. He traveled to Achaia to preach. Corinth was the capital of Achaia, so he walked into exactly the same audiences the apostle Paul had. Initially Apollos only knew part of the gospel. But "after Priscilla and Aquila heard him, they took him home and explained the way of God to him more accurately" (Acts 18:26). With his newfound knowledge, Apollos preached the same kind of message but with his own style.

We get a good glimpse into human nature as Paul later addressed the believers in Corinth. They responded to those who came and preached to them by forming warring camps. The people then reacted much like we react today. We tend to compare Christian leaders and fall into camps behind our choices. We must make a concerted effort to avoid doing so. Each of us could cite an example, but every branch of in-depth Bible study has loyal supporters who swear by that particular method or teacher. Some would rather fight than switch.

God is wooing people to His table for the meat of His Word like never before. He is joyfully using many different methods and styles to accomplish His goal of equipping His church to be effective and holy during difficult days. God has raised many fine teachers and preachers for our day. Let's reap the benefit of as many as possible and value their contributions whether they are magnetic like Apollos, analytical like Luke, forthright like Paul, or warm like Priscilla and Aquila. Paul's style may have been one reason some of the Corinthians preferred Apollos: Paul didn't mince words. But his answer to those who were camping around certain speakers? "Oh, grow up!" (see 1 Cor. 3:3–4).

Praying God's Word Today

In the wise words of the apostle Paul, we know that "neither the one who plants nor the one who waters is anything, but only God who gives the growth" (1 Cor. 3:7). May my focus be so entirely upon You—on the Holy Spirit, who is faithful to guide us into all the truth (John 16:13)—that You will protect me from ever being deceived into embracing a different gospel (Gal. 1:6). I cling to Your Word, Lord, and find confidence in Your way.

Day 42

Spiritual Questions

BEFORE YOU BEGIN

Read Acts 19:1–7

STOP AND CONSIDER

"Did you receive the Holy Spirit when you believed?"

"No," they told him, "we haven't even heard that there is a Holy Spirit." (v. 2)

What do you do with those knotty doctrinal questions, ones with outspoken proponents on either side? How do you deal with things you don't understand?

What do you notice about churches and individuals who are vocally, vehemently staunch about matters that go far beyond the essentials?

Acts 19 begins with Paul's meeting an interesting group of believers. They did not know about the Holy Spirit, and they had received only the baptism of John. These people were in a strange situation—in limbo between the Old and New Testaments. Paul told them of Christ with the result that they received the Holy Spirit, spoke in tongues, and prophesied.

These original converts knew virtually nothing about the Holy Spirit. Even their knowledge of the Old Testament didn't help much because the Spirit's activity was so different after the coming of Christ. Remember, only about a hundred people in the Old Testament were ever described as having the Holy Spirit in or on them. Prior to Christ and the birth of the New Testament church, the Spirit's purpose was not to mark salvation but to empower certain individuals for designated tasks. Since the birth of the church, the Holy Spirit takes up residence in every believer in Christ (see Rom. 8:9). John's baptism was a sign of repentance in anticipation of the coming Christ. Christian baptism is a mark to demonstrate the salvation Christ has given and the receipt of the Holy Spirit.

God knew the concept of the Holy Spirit would be difficult for new believers to understand as He raised up His church, so God made His Spirit obvious. He sometimes accompanied His Spirit with a sudden physical evidence such as speaking in tongues. Few topics have caused division like speaking in tongues. But no matter what you believe about tongues, Paul was clear on at least two points concerning the activity of the Holy Spirit:

1. All believers are baptized by the Holy Spirit. The Spirit resides in all believers equally (see 1 Cor. 12:13).
2. Not all believers spoke in tongues (see 1 Cor. 12:30).

Many believe God never uses the gift of tongues today. Many others believe God always gives the gift of tongues to every true believer. I believe we are wise to avoid words like *always* and *never.* He told us to love one another, not judge one another.

Praying God's Word Today

Father, how I pray that no one will be able to deceive us with empty arguments, for because of these things Your wrath is coming on the disobedient (Eph. 5:6). Rather, may our believing hearts be joined together in love, so that we may have all the riches of assured understanding, and have the knowledge of Your mystery—Jesus Christ—for in Him all the treasures of wisdom and knowledge are hidden (Col. 2:2–3).

Day 43

Rewards of Discipleship

Before You Begin

Read Acts 19:8–10

Stop and Consider

When some became hardened and would not believe, slandering the Way in front of the crowd, he withdrew from them and met separately with the disciples. (v. 9)

What have you gleaned from an intense season (or perhaps a lifetime) of discipleship that would never have been yours any other way? ______

As you continue to grow in Christ, how could you be more deliberate about discipling others, beginning with your own children? ______

Acts 19:8–10 summarizes Paul's ministry in Ephesus, where he preached in the synagogue for three months until stiff opposition arose, persuading Paul to move his ministry to a lecture hall where he could concentrate on discipling believers, with the result that "all the inhabitants of the province of Asia, both Jews and Greeks, heard the word of the Lord" (v. 10).

Interestingly, it was the same group in Ephesus that had previously asked Paul to spend more time with them (see Acts 18:20) who quickly got over him when he returned! "Some became hardened and would not believe" (19:9), which is why Paul took a group of the followers aside and began discipling them daily. Can you imagine being part of that Bible study? But again, don't miss the bountiful fruit produced from Paul's discipleship group: within two years the message of Jesus Christ and His gospel had spread throughout the entire region. The churches of Laodicea, Colosse, and Hierapolis were all founded as a result of this great and supernatural movement of God.

Like Gideon's army (see Judg. 7), a few well-trained soldiers in the Lord's service can be more effective than hundreds who have never been discipled. God honors His Word and often overtly blesses discipleship with fruit far beyond human effort. Paul was an effective teacher, but God still produced fruit far beyond his labor. When a few seeds produce a huge crop, God's up to something supernatural! Acknowledge it and praise Him! He makes obvious His blessing on true discipleship.

God performs His work in countless ways we cannot see. He remains active in our lives even when we are unaware, even when we feel defeated, unwelcome, and misunderstood. Sometimes, however, He makes Himself entirely obvious—as He would go on to work through Paul in the passage we'll consider tomorrow—so that what we see will strengthen our faith in what we cannot see. The early church was learning concepts completely new to most. God purposely showed His visible handprints so that many would place their lives in His invisible hands.

Praying God's Word Today

Since we have been forewarned of the dangers of biblical ignorance, help us to be on our guard so we are not led away by the error of the immoral and fall from our own stability. Grow us, precious Father, in the grace and knowledge of our Lord and Savior Jesus Christ. To Him be the glory both now and to the day of eternity. Amen (2 Pet. 3:17–18).

Day 44

The Perfect Storm

Before You Begin

Read Acts 19:11–20

Stop and Consider

This became known to everyone who lived in Ephesus, both Jews and Greeks. Then fear fell on all of them, and the name of the Lord Jesus was magnified. (v. 17)

Many quibble over the authenticity and availability of miracles today. But what is God's purpose behind His miracles, and what should be our ultimate goal in seeking them?

What would you give for a present-day experience of fear falling on all of us and the name of Jesus being widely magnified? What would it likely take for such an event to occur?

My oldest daughter, Amanda, was very frightened of storms when she was little. Loud peals of thunder sent her into near panic, even when we were in the safety of our home. One day when the sky seemed to be falling, I held her in my arms and said, "Honey, the heavens are just displaying the glory of God (see Ps. 19:1). They are showing us how mighty He is." Her little forehead furrowed as if she were really thinking over what I had said. Some weeks later, she was upstairs playing when a storm hit. I heard her feet scurry like lightning down the stairs. Then she yelled at the top of her lungs, "Mommy! God's really showing off today!"

God seemed to work overtime on Paul's stop in Ephesus as He revealed His power in extraordinary ways. God used special demonstrations to authenticate His ambassadors and persuade belief. More than anywhere else in the apostolic era, it was a time when God chose to display His power. The accent of Acts 19 appears in verse 11: "God was performing extraordinary miracles by Paul's hands."

One reason God showed His marvelous power to such a degree in this particular city was because Ephesus was a renowned center for magical incantations. In his book *Paul the Traveller*, Ernle Bradford wrote, "Ephesus was the centre of occult studies, indeed it has been called 'The Home of Magic.'" He also tells us, "Ephesus was full of wizards, sorcerers, witches, astrologers, diviners of the entrails of animals, and people who could read one's fortune by the palm of the hand or the fall of knucklebones."[12] Many of the Ephesians were neck deep in the occult, but virtually the entire population was extremely interested in supernatural phenomena and the powers of the unseen world. This is one reason Paul was most outspoken to them about spiritual warfare in his letter to them, the book of Ephesians. While Paul was in their midst, God intentionally got their attention by surpassing anything they had ever seen.

I believe God revealed His power there to make true repentance obvious. The activity of the Holy Spirit in Acts 19:18–19 is perhaps my favorite of those that God performed in Ephesus—only slightly more awe-inspiring than the power in Paul's facecloths and work aprons, or the hilarious story of the seven sons of a Jewish priest named Sceva in verses 14–15. (I can hardly read that story without laughing. I'm sure God has a great sense of humor. This account makes me wonder if the devil may even have one.) Some works of God are more subtle but not necessarily less supernatural. According to John 16:8, one of the most important activities of the Spirit is to "convict the world about sin, righteousness, and judgment." Matthew 3:8 tells us to "produce fruit consistent with repentance." And when the new converts burned their sorcery books, they brought forth some impressive fruit!

> God wants to be found. He does not will for any to miss Him, and He is gracious to show up where we are looking.

God can reveal Himself through both natural or supernatural means. Both are at His complete disposal. Although God also worked in subtle ways, He apparently chose to reveal Himself through several phenomenal means while Paul was in Ephesus. Why did He make His activity so obvious among the Ephesians? Because Satan had made his work so obvious there. Satan is powerful, but he is no match for the Almighty God.

Sometimes I am completely perplexed by God's willingness to humor us. His mercy knows no bounds. When He wanted to lead the Magi to the Christ child, He did not lead them by a mark in the sand. He led them through a star because they were stargazers—then He went beyond anything they had ever seen. In the same way, when God wanted to lead the Ephesians to the Savior, He did not lead them through a cloudy pillar. He got their attention through supernatural phenomena, because that's where they were looking. God wants to be found. He does not will for any to miss Him, and He is so gracious to show up right where we are looking—so He can take us beyond anything we've ever seen.

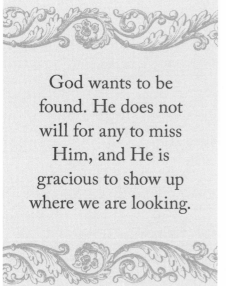

God sometimes reveals Himself to a homeless man hiding under a bridge through a blanket brought to him by a caring minister. He sometimes reveals Himself to a drunk through a servant who cares for him and offers him Living Water. He sometimes reveals Himself to a prostitute through a godly police officer who tells her Christ can set her free.

If we're waiting for the needy to walk through our church doors, we may wait a long time. God doesn't wait for people to come to Him. He goes to them and desires to intervene right at the point of their need. He's looking for a few brave people, like the apostle Paul, who are willing to go rather than wait for them to come. He's not looking for show-offs. He's looking for people through whom He can show off His Son. May we be some of those people. We might end up agreeing with Amanda: "God's really showing off today!"

How has God personalized His revelation of Himself to you? Think of an example when He met you at a particular point of need, showing His complete knowledge both of you and your situation. What are some of the things this tells you about Him? ____________

Praying God's Word Today

I receive Paul's prayer for the Ephesians as my own today, asking that You would give me a spirit of wisdom and revelation in the knowledge of You. I pray that the eyes of my heart may be enlightened so I may know what is the hope of Your calling, what are the glorious riches of Your inheritance among the saints, and what is the immeasurable greatness of Your power to us who believe, according to the working of Your vast strength. You demonstrated this power in the Messiah by raising Him from the dead and seating Him at Your right hand in the heavens—far above every ruler and authority, power and dominion, and every title given, not only in this age but also in the one to come (Eph. 1:17–21).

Day 45

For Love or Money

Before You Begin

Read Acts 19:21–31

Stop and Consider

"So not only do we run a risk that our business may be discredited, but also that the temple of the great goddess Artemis may be despised." (v. 27)

Think of a common misconception you hear raised against Christianity in our day. What are some of the holes in that particular argument?

In what way does money or a certain level of lifestyle corrupt a person's openness to the gospel? How does (or how should) Christianity threaten our natural wants and attitudes?

While Paul was in Ephesus, the Emperor Claudius was poisoned and the Roman Empire fell into the hands of a seventeen-year-old boy named Nero. Christians soon suspected he was the Antichrist. Rome would ultimately be an important part of Paul's life. His wisdom told him to go there. God did not want him to miss it either, so He placed a virtually irresistible compulsion in Paul. And just in case the motivations of wisdom and burden were not enough, we are about to see a third: trouble—lots of trouble.

In the passages we've read so far, Paul was opposed only once before by the Gentiles. The first case of opposition occurred in Philippi (Acts 16:16–19) when Paul cast the demon from the fortune-telling girl. Now here in Acts 19 a silversmith named Demetrius stirred up opposition because the Christian revival was a threat to the income of those who sold idols. In both Philippi and Ephesus, it was profit that motivated Gentiles to oppose Paul.

Obviously a person does not have to be entirely genuine to be effective! Demetrius appealed to the people of Ephesus both financially with the claim that Paul was hurting trade, and spiritually with the idea that he was robbing Artemis of her majesty. Demetrius apparently reasoned that one of those two needles would surely hit a vein in everyone within earshot. He may have lacked integrity, but he didn't lack intelligence. His approach worked better than he could have dreamed. The people began shouting, "Great is Artemis of the Ephesians!"

In Greek mythology Artemis was believed to be the daughter of Zeus. The temple the Ephesians had built in her honor was so mammoth, it was later considered one of the Seven Wonders of the Ancient World. The Ephesians exceeded the size of her temple, however, with their ability to make a buck in her name. The silver craftsmen were making a fortune off silver charms and statuettes of her likeness. You can be fairly certain most of the merchants cared very little about robbing Artemis of her majesty. You can also be certain the outspoken apostle had assured them she had none.

This scene must have been something to behold. The crowd shouted "Great is Artemis of the Ephesians" for hours. Paul wanted to go into the theater to speak to the crowd, but his friends persuaded him not to go. In the situation I find a number of fascinating clues into the person and personality of Paul.

1. Based on Paul's willingness to address the crowd (v. 30), we may assume that he sometimes had more courage than sense! He was going to speak out in behalf of Christianity no matter what! The theater in Ephesus held twenty-five thousand people! When God gives us good sense, He expects us to use it. I believe the only time we are to walk into a dangerous or risky situation is when we have crystal clear leadership from God.

> Paul could be tough, and he could be very gracious. He was not so different from the rest of us, perhaps, on any given day.

2. Also based on verse 30, I believe Paul's disciples were not afraid to disagree with him. He was not a religious dictator who surrounded himself with yes-men. Times obviously existed when his colleagues said no. He was not only a preacher and teacher, he was a discussion leader (see v. 9). Leaders who are afraid of others disagreeing with them usually don't leave much room for discussion.

3. I am fairly impressed by a third assumption we can make: Paul sometimes let the wisdom of others take precedence over his own desires. We read that Paul's friends would not let him go. If I know anything at all about the apostle, he had to let them not let him! Short of being physically tied down, I can't imagine how they could stop him from going unless he submitted to their wisdom. He could have rebuked them for not believing that speaking up was worth the risk of dying. Instead he obviously listened to them and relented. I am refreshed by leaders who do not think they always have to be right.

4. One more assumption I would like to make is based on verse 31. Paul obviously had many good friends. When we began our journey together, I'm not sure any of us pictured Paul as friendly. Although he possessed a passion for Christ and a perseverance

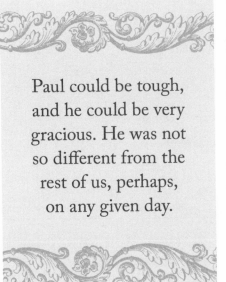

in servitude, I never really thought of him as being genuinely gracious. I assumed he was respected far more than he was liked. But Paul obviously had good friends from every walk of life: Jews, Gentiles, rich, and poor. Aquila and Priscilla did not leave their home and travel with Paul because he was unpleasant! Obviously he possessed a genuinely likable personality. Many people surrendered to serve Christ as a direct result of Paul's influence. Had he been an ogre, people would not have been so ready to follow his example.

Verse 31 describes another group of people who were extremely fond of Paul: officials of the province. They loved him enough to beg him not to venture into the theater. Let's learn something about judging others. We tend to describe people in brief phrases: he's always funny; she's always so bossy; he's such a controlling person; she never fails to be upbeat. God created human beings to be the most complex creatures alive. None of us can be wrapped up in a single phrase. Yes, Paul could be unyielding, but he could also be persuaded. He could be tough, and he could be very gracious. He was not so different from the rest of us, perhaps, on any given day!

Which of these four assumptions intrigues or surprises you the most about Paul? Which needs to be more descriptive of you as well? ______________________________

____

____

____

____

____

Praying God's Word Today

Lord, how well I know that I, too, was once darkness, but now I am light in the Lord. Help me, then, to walk as a child of light—for the fruit of the light results in all goodness, righteousness, and truth—discerning what is pleasing to You. May I not participate in the fruitless works of darkness, but instead, expose them (Eph. 5:8–11), being wise about what is good, yet innocent about what is evil (Rom. 16:19).

Day 46

What Are You Fighting For?

Before You Begin

Read Acts 19:32–41

Stop and Consider

Meanwhile, some were shouting one thing and some another, because the assembly was in confusion, and most of them did not know why they had come together. (v. 32)

Have you ever been part of a large opposition or protest group? What are some of the negative offshoots that can occur, even when the reason behind the uprising is valid?

Have you ever violated your own conscience or beliefs because you were angry or opposed to something—perhaps because you'd come for a fight and weren't leaving without one?

The crowd of twenty-five thousand Ephesians was a madhouse. That's when the Jews pushed a man named Alexander to the front, hoping to provide a defense, a disclaimer for them. They wanted him to tell the crowds that Paul's teaching was separate from theirs, that they were not responsible for the financial harm done to the silver craftsmen. "But when they recognized that he was a Jew, a united cry went up from all of them for about two hours: 'Great is Artemis of the Ephesians!'" (Acts 19:34).

The Jews knew without a doubt that the silver craftsmen were profiting off the ignorance and sinful practices of pagans. They certainly had a stake in confronting idolatry. Exodus 20:3–4 unmistakably forbids it. Because of their opposition to Paul, however, they violated their own consciences and belief system.

Consider, though, the beliefs of the Ephesians. They believed the image of Artemis had fallen from heaven. Some scholars assume they were describing a meteor that had hit Ephesus, one that the people had thought to look like a multi-breasted woman. Therefore, they assumed it was the goddess Artemis and hailed her as the deity of childbirth. I am sometimes amazed at the things people believe.

A number of years ago, I prepared to teach the book of Genesis in Sunday school. In an attempt to be prepared for questions and rebuttals, I thought I'd study the theory of evolution. I was somewhat intimidated by the prospect, but I checked out a few books and started my research. I only had to flip a few pages before my chin dropped to the ground. At times I even laughed out loud. I couldn't believe that this theory is taught as fact in many public schools. After a fairly in-depth comparison, I decided it took far more faith to believe in evolution than creation!

When Paul came to Ephesus, he brought the message of a Messiah sent from God who offers eternal life to every individual who believes. I'm no rocket scientist, but I find Paul's message far more believable than a goddess falling out of heaven in the form of a meteor. Yes, God requires faith—but not as much as a number of other belief systems falling out of the skies today. Go ahead and believe Him. He's very believable.

PRAYING GOD'S WORD TODAY

Father, You warn us in Your Word that if anyone teaches other doctrine and does not agree with the sound teaching of our Lord Jesus Christ and with the teaching that promotes godliness, he is conceited, understanding nothing, but having a sick interest in disputes and arguments over words. From these come envy, quarreling, slanders, evil suspicions, and constant disagreement among men whose minds are depraved and deprived of the truth, who imagine that godliness is a way to material gain (1 Tim. 6:3–5). O Lord, give me clarity of mind and biblical perspective when it comes to my beliefs, as well as a heart of discernment and compassion for those who disagree.

Day 47

Give Me a Break

BEFORE YOU BEGIN

Read Acts 20:1–12

STOP AND CONSIDER

A young man named Eutychus was sitting on a window sill and sank into a deep sleep as Paul kept on speaking. . . . Overcome by sleep he fell down from the third story. (v. 9)

Here around the halfway point of this book, I feel like taking a quick breather, and this story is a good place to do it. What's the funniest thing you ever saw happen in church?

The young man Eutychus—do you think he ever outgrew this story? What's it like to be forever immortalized in certain circles for some silly or embarrassing thing you once did?

I am so amused by this text. God used my desire to be like Paul to motivate me to write this book. So far, I've noticed that most of the characteristics I share with him are those of his human rather than his spiritual nature. A common colloquialism states, "If the shoe fits, wear it." I don't know what size shoe you wear, but I can tell you in advance: this lesson is a size 7 medium. Just my size. Read on. It just may come in your size too.

In two verses Luke tells us that after leaving Ephesus, Paul then traveled through Macedonia and into Greece where he stayed three months. The Jews again plotted against him as he prepared to sail for Syria, so he took the land route back through Macedonia once more. Counting Luke, eight people accompanied Paul back through Macedonia.

The group spent a week in Troas, culminating in the event I find so humorous and convicting. Paul taught, and because they were going to leave the next day, he talked until midnight. Luke tells us that the upstairs room where they were meeting contained many lamps. A young man named Eutychus fell asleep, fell out the window, "and was picked up dead" (Acts 20:9).

You know you aren't having a good day when you fall asleep in church and are picked up dead. Unlike most of us, however, Eutychus stayed dead for only a short while.

Luke wrote meticulously without inclusion of unnecessary details. What bearing do you suppose the lamps had on the account of the midnight meeting? And while we are supposing, can you think of any reasons why God made certain Luke joined Paul in time for this strange set of circumstances?

We want to grasp as accurately as possible the kind of man Paul was. The love of Christ so compelled him that his energy seemed to have no bounds. We will do his memory no harm, however, by pointing out that sometimes his energy exceeded that of his audience. Like many other preachers and teachers, Paul preached longer than his audience was prepared to listen!

Figuratively speaking, at this point I am pulling the shoe out of the box and putting it on my guilty foot. A woman once said to me after one of my lectures, "I'm going home and taking a nap. You've worn me out." Sometimes those of us in teaching, preaching, and speaking positions talk too long. Mind you, we can have the best of intentions. I can entirely relate to the apostle for being so long-winded; this was his last chance, and he was determined to say everything he could before he departed. He didn't want to leave a single thing unsaid.

> Paul didn't always know when to wrap up a message. Don't you get a kick out of Luke's words: "Paul talked on and on"?

In Paul's defense, I must explain one of the pitfalls accompanying the gift of teaching. Teachers often feel that whatever they learn, they must teach—every last word of it! I have forty-five minutes on Sunday mornings during which I often try to teach everything I learned in hours of preparation. Sometimes I've tried to teach all I knew—plus a lot of things I didn't! Paul obviously didn't always know when to wrap up a message either. Don't you get a kick out of Luke's words: "Paul talked on and on"? (v. 9 NIV).

I believe God purposely gave us the opportunity to giggle over a fairly typical event: a preacher or teacher outlasting the audience. However, God provided a very effective eye-opener by doing something quite atypical. He gave Paul a chance to raise the dead!

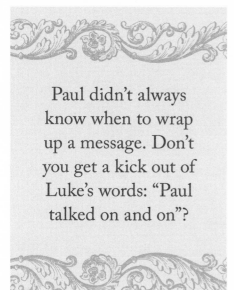

Picture the scene with me a moment. A large group of people were gathered in one room, and the lamps provided just enough heat to make the atmosphere cozy and warm. Most of the listeners had awakened with the rising sun, and the time was now approaching midnight. Eutychus was sitting in the windowsill, trying to stay attentive. The young man's eyelids would drop; then he would force them open. He finally fell into a deep sleep, probably had a dream that caused him to jump, and out the window he flew. This story would not be humorous without the happy ending. Since you know God raised Eutychus from the dead, wouldn't you have loved to see Paul's face when the boy fell out of the window? He ran downstairs as fast as his legs could carry him. "Paul . . . threw himself on the young man and put his arms around him. 'Don't be alarmed,' he said, 'He's alive!'" (v. 10 NIV). What a relief! A wonderfully rare phenomenon took place that day.

I find myself amused once again as the scene ends. Paul went back to business as usual. He climbed three flights of stairs, broke bread with them, and talked until daylight. All in a day's work. I have a feeling no one fell asleep this time. In fact, they may have been wide awake for days! Here is my moral to the story: may God bring back to life whom man hath put to sleep.

So make me one promise as we conclude: never sit close to a window when working on one of my lessons, listening to one of my teaching series, or reading one of my books. Meanwhile, I'll see if I can get this size 7 shoe off my foot and back in the box where it belongs.

Another interesting side of Paul, huh? After all this time we've spent studying his life, what do you find most inspiring about him? Most puzzling? Most interesting? Most refreshing?

Praying God's Word Today

Lord, Your precepts are right, making the heart glad; Your commandment is radiant, making the eyes light up (Ps. 19:8). Your Word is a constant source of delight and renewal. So today I thank You for filling me from the abundance of Your house and letting me drink from Your refreshing stream, for with You is life's fountain. In Your light I see light (Ps. 36:8–9). In Your Word, I find all I ever need, right when I need it.

Day 48

Time Together

Before You Begin

Read Acts 20:13–21

Stop and Consider

"I testified to both Jews and Greeks about repentance toward God and faith in our Lord Jesus." (v. 21)

What bonds have you developed with those you've grown close to at church or in some other Christian environment? How do these connections compare with others you've had?

What do you think are the most significant reasons why pastors don't typically stay long in any one place? What does time do to the relationship between a church and its leaders?

After his eventful night in Troas, Paul set sail on his journey toward Jerusalem. He purposely sailed past Ephesus, yet he summoned the elders to come to Miletus and meet with him. Paul had little time, so he left the Ephesian elders the basic necessities.

Like a father with only a few moments left to share his heart with his children, Paul shared things that were priority to him. He reminded them of the attention he had given to their needs. He shared his assumptions, his ambition, his heartfelt admonition, and his deep affection. He said, "You know, from the first day I set foot in Asia, how I was with you the whole time—serving the Lord with all humility, with tears, and with the trials that came to me through the plots of the Jews—and that I did not shrink back from proclaiming to you anything that was profitable, or from teaching it to you in public and from house to house" (Acts 20:18–20).

I believe Paul was personally attentive to the Ephesians because he became involved with them emotionally as well as spiritually. Remember, he remained among these people for several years. I believe he poured himself out among them as much or more than any other group to whom he ministered. They saw his "humility." This word involves "the confession of his sin and a deep realization of his unworthiness to receive God's marvelous grace." He was open with them about his past sin and his feelings of unworthiness in the ministry God had given him. They not only saw his humility; they saw his heart. He did not hide from them his tears or the pain of his hardships.

The Ephesians knew Paul was genuine. He approached them withholding nothing. He did not hesitate to preach anything that would be helpful. He loved them enough to teach them anything and everything that would be of benefit, even if they didn't like it. He was willing to hurt their feelings momentarily if it would help their hearts eternally.

Paul had given them everything he had while he was there. In verse 27, he restated: "I did not shrink back from declaring to you the whole plan of God." He didn't just teach them the many wonderful things God wanted to do for them. He also taught them the truth about hardships that would inevitably come and the calling of the crucified life.

Praying God's Word Today

I remember that Paul told the church in Thessalonica, "We cared so much for you that we were pleased to share with you not only the gospel of God but also our own lives, because you had become dear to us" (1 Thess. 2:8). Father, may my love for Your church—my brothers and sisters—be this real and authentic, not staying away from our meetings, as some habitually do, but encouraging each other, and all the more as we see the day drawing near (Heb. 10:25).

Day 49

Survival Is Optional

BEFORE YOU BEGIN

Read Acts 20:22–24

STOP AND CONSIDER

In town after town the Holy Spirit testifies to me
that chains and afflictions are waiting for me. (v. 23)

We know from previous passages that Paul knew a closed door when he saw one. Why did the pronouncement of verse 23 not qualify as one? ______

What gives a person the confidence to wade into this kind of buzz saw? Was Paul not afraid of it? Did he have some kind of immunity to fear? ______

In his attentiveness Paul withheld nothing from the Ephesians. He assumed he was bound to have difficulties when he got to Jerusalem because the Holy Spirit had warned him of hardships in every other city. He couldn't imagine Jerusalem being any exception. In fact, he probably assumed he would have more problems than ever as he returned to Jerusalem.

He also assumed he would never see the Ephesians again. I have a feeling he might have feared he would be put to death in Jerusalem. Some scholars believe he did see the Ephesians once more. Others believe he did not. At this point he spoke to them as if he would never see them again.

Next he shared with them his chief ambition: "I count my life of no value to myself, so that I may finish my course and the ministry I received from the Lord Jesus" (Acts 20:24). He was so determined to be faithful to the task God had assigned him, his certainty of suffering could not dissuade him.

Fear is a very powerful tool. Don't think for a moment Satan did not try to use fear to hinder the apostle from fulfilling God's purposes, and don't think Paul was not terrified at times. Of course he was. To think otherwise would be to minimize his faithfulness. Paul was afraid, but his love for Christ exceeded his fear of suffering and death. His primary ambition was finishing his task faithfully. Notice the phrase in verse 24: "the ministry I received from the Lord Jesus." Paul felt no responsibility to complete the task Christ had given Peter or Barnabas or Timothy. He believed and taught that God has specific plans for each believer. He expressed the concept clearly in Ephesians 2:10: "We are His creation—created in Christ Jesus for good works, which God prepared ahead of time so that we should walk in them."

God has a task for you—one He planned very long ago and suited for our present generation. Remember you are not responsible for completing anyone else's task, just yours. God desires for us to encourage one another in our tasks (see Heb. 10:24–25), but we are responsible only for completing our own.

Praying God's Word Today

Lord, I never want to go looking for trouble, but I desire the change of heart that enables me to rejoice in afflictions because I know that affliction produces endurance, endurance produces proven character, and proven character produces hope. And this hope does not disappoint, because Your love has been poured out in our hearts through the Holy Spirit who was given to us (Rom. 5:3–5). By endurance we gain our lives (Luke 21:19). Strengthen my character to embrace any hardship that brings You ultimate glory.

Day 50

No Easy Way to Say This

Before You Begin

Read Acts 20:25–38

Stop and Consider

"And now I commit you to God and to the message of His grace, which is able to build you up and to give you an inheritance among all who are sanctified." (v. 32)

It's hard to say good-bye to those we love, even if we know the time has come to go our separate ways. What have you learned from past experiences with farewells?

What sphere of responsibility has God given you in your home, church, or community—people who look to you for help and example? What is required of you to give it to them?

Believing he would never see the Ephesians again, Paul had an urgency to share with them an admonition. He warned the Ephesian elders about the vulnerability of the young church. He told them to expect savage wolves to try to devour the flock. Paul considered the warning so vital, he repeated it over and over during the three years he was among them.

Don't miss an important part of his admonition. In verse 28, Paul named two groups the elders were to keep watch over: themselves and the flock God had given them. What an important message Paul's words send to us! We can hardly keep watch over a group if we don't keep watch over ourselves! The Greek term for "keep watch" is *prosecho*. "As a nautical term, it means to hold a ship in a direction, to sail towards . . . to hold on one's course toward a place." Many leaders have seasons when their lives seem temporarily out of control. Most people who have served God for decades have had a season in which they got off course. Those who never depart from the course in many years of service deserve our highest commendations, but they are rare.

I do not believe a leader who temporarily veers away from the course should never be allowed to lead again. I can't find a biblical precedent for such thinking. On the other hand, we are wise leaders to step out of leadership when we are having a difficult time staying on the course. We simply cannot lead others to a place to which we are not steering our own lives. Yes, leaders must watch over their own lives very carefully, but Paul also told them they must act like shepherds keeping watch over their flocks.

We don't have to be church elders for these words and warnings to apply to us. If God has assigned you a flock, you have a serious responsibility to keep a close watch over your own life and to care deeply for theirs. A crucial part of keeping watch over our flocks is knowing the Word of God! In verse 30, Paul warned that "men will arise and distort the truth" (NIV). The word "distort" denotes an action of twisting or turning. Satan is a master at twisting and turning the Word of God. He's been honing his twisting skills since his first successful attempt in the Garden of Eden. He subtly twists the Word in hope that we won't realize we've been misled until after he wreaks havoc. Paul had very little time to address the Ephesian elders, yet the warning to watch over themselves and their flocks was an absolute priority.

> He was the one who taught others, "Love never fails." I wonder if at this moment he thought love also never fails to hurt.

Paul shared one last element with the Ephesians. He shared his sincere affection for them. The final picture painted at the end of Acts 20 touches my heart so much. Paul was a man of many words, but the primary message of his affection for the Ephesians came more in action than in words. Any man as beloved as Paul had most assuredly loved. He was the very one who taught others, "Love never fails" (1 Cor. 13:8 NIV). I wonder if at this moment he thought love also never fails to hurt. He committed them to God, said a few last words, then knelt with them and prayed.

Don't quickly pass by this moment. Let it take form in your mind. Imagine a group of men, replete with all the things that make them men—size, stature, strength, controlled emotions—on their knees praying together. Thankfully this is not a picture I have trouble imagining. My pastor often asks the men of our church to join him at the altar down on their knees in prayer. As a woman in the church, nothing makes me feel more secure. To me, a man is his tallest when he is down on his knees in prayer.

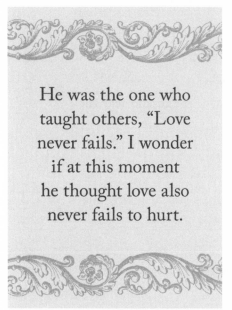

Imagine this next scene between Paul and the elders: "There was a great deal of weeping by everyone. And embracing Paul, they kissed him" (v. 37). One by one each man hugged him and said good-bye. With every embrace I'm sure he remembered something special—a good laugh shared, a late night over a sick loved one, a baptism in a cold river, a heated argument resolved. He had been their shepherd. Now he would leave them to tend their flocks on their own. In the midst of painful good-byes, perhaps Paul thought the same thing I've thought a time or two when my heart was hurting: "I will never let myself get this involved again." But of course, he did. And so will we, if we continue to walk in the footsteps of our Savior. To extend hands of service without hearts of love is virtually meaningless.

The chapter concludes with Paul and his friends walking side by side down the path to the docks, beards still wet with tears. Had I been Paul, I would have gotten on that ship as quickly as possible and dared not look back. That's not what happened. Luke opens the next chapter by reporting, "We tore ourselves away from them and set sail" (21:1). I think Luke, who was waiting at the boat (see 20:13), literally had to go and tear the apostle away from them.

Obviously the Ephesians had some idea how blessed they were to have the kind of leader Paul was to them. He was a leader who kept watch over himself and his followers. In nautical terms, he was the best kind of captain—one who kept the vessel on course even if his compass took him far from those he loved. He had given them all he had. The best kind of good-bye is the kind with no regrets.

What might be some parting words or themes you'd like to leave behind to those who follow you? What are the most important warnings and encouragements to pass on?

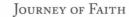

Praying God's Word Today

When it all comes down, Lord, my prayer is that we, Your people—through Your mercy—will present our bodies as a living sacrifice, holy and pleasing to You; this is our spiritual worship. May we not be conformed to this age, but be transformed by the renewing of our minds, so that we may discern Your good, pleasing, and perfect will (Rom. 12:1–2).

Day 51

Hospitality House

Before You Begin

Read Acts 21:1–6

Stop and Consider

All of them, with their wives and children, escorted us out of the city. After kneeling down on the beach to pray, we said good-bye to one another. (vv. 5–6)

Have you ever encountered a person who had reason to be cold toward you but responded warmly instead? Is there someone you should surprise with an unexpected gift of grace?

How do you interpret the disciples' telling Paul "through the Spirit" (v. 4) not to go to Jerusalem? How can we tell the difference between a heavy heart and the Lord's will?

Although Paul had the opportunity to stretch his legs at several ports on his way to Jerusalem, he disembarked twice for a number of days. His first lengthy stop was not by choice. Because the first boat made so many stops, the traveling preachers sought out a vessel going straight across to Phoenicia (Acts 21:2), hoping to save time. To their dismay the ship docked in Tyre for seven days to unload cargo. Have you ever noticed how often God has a blessing on the unscheduled stops along our way? God had a blessing waiting for Paul and the others on their unscheduled stop.

Verse 4 tells us that Paul sought out the Christian disciples in Tyre so that he and his men would have a place to stay. Acts 11:19 tells how Christians had been planted in Phoenicia, the region in which Tyre was located. They were scattered by the same wave of persecution in which Stephen was martyred.

Don't forget how deeply Paul, then known as Saul, had been involved in the persecution that caused these believers to scatter. Had they heard about the amazing convert, or did they believe he was still a terrible threat? Either way, they were surprised to lay eyes on the sea-weary travelers. I never cease to be amazed at the hospitality of believers in the New Testament church. Even in my grandmother's day, she and many others often opened their homes to total strangers who needed a place to rest for a night on their long travels. I am saddened by our loss of hospitality today. The disciples in Phoenicia opened their homes to Paul and his fellow travelers. Their hearts were so instantly bound with his, they begged him not to go to Jerusalem.

This time, entire families of believers accompanied him to the harbor. Can you imagine what a sight this scene must have been for others to behold? Men, women, and children kneeling in the sand praying with one heart and mind for the apostle and his beloved associates. Just picture what the sand must have looked like after Paul boarded the ship and the crowd went back home. Footprints leading to and from the shore. Then nothing but knee prints clustered together in the damp sand. A sight for God to behold. Long after the tide washed away every print, the power of those prayers was still at work.

Praying God's Word Today

Lord, may I be one who practices brotherly love continually, not neglecting to show hospitality, knowing that by doing this some have welcomed angels as guests without knowing it. May I remember the prisoners, as though I were in prison with them, and the mistreated, as though I myself were suffering bodily (Heb. 13:1–3). Help me to be a person who cares, who loves, who overlooks, who warmly receives—a person who truly loves my neighbor as myself (Matt. 22:39) that I might bring glory to You.

Day 52

Prophecies and Problems

Before You Begin

Read Acts 21:7–14

Stop and Consider

Since he would not be persuaded, we stopped talking
and simply said, "The Lord's will be done!" (v. 14)

Have you experienced a time when someone desperately wanted you to do something that you could not do, out of conscience, out of conviction? How did that affect you?

Have you begged and pleaded with God for something you know you're not going to get? What should your reaction be when the answer is a fairly definite no?

Acts 21:8 tells us Paul and the others disembarked in Caesarea and stayed in the house of Philip. Philip is first mentioned in Acts 6:5 in the list of the seven original deacons. Not only was he a Spirit-filled Christian and a very wise man, he was also an extremely effective evangelist. We can compile something of a profile based on Acts 8:26–40. When we see his faithfulness, it is no wonder he had four daughters who prophesied. We considered the rich heritage Timothy received from his mother and grandmother. Philip's faithfulness obviously had a similar effect on his daughters.

Young people are far more likely to surrender their lives to serve God when they've seen genuine examples firsthand. Many are touched by the faithfulness of youth ministers, Sunday school teachers, and pastors, but nothing can match the lasting impact of a faithful parent. If my children don't think I'm genuine, no one else's opinion matters to me. On the front page of my Bible, I've written a reminder I'm forced to see every time I open it: "No amount of success in ministry will make up for failure at home."

What do you think Paul made of these four women who prophesied? You may be wondering if he had to be resuscitated when he met them. In his defense I would like to say that Paul was the first to recognize women with the gift of prophecy (when he taught spiritual gifts in 1 Cor. 11). A study of the entire life and ministry of Paul reveals an interesting fact. He had a vastly different outlook and attitude toward women than many people suppose. Unfortunately many people have based their thinking about him on a couple of excerpts from his writings. Knowing Paul, if he had disapproved of Philip's four daughters, he would have been the first to tell him!

What exactly were Philip's daughters doing anyway? What does prophesying mean? The original word is *propheteuo*, which means "to declare truths through the inspiration of God's Holy Spirit . . . to tell forth God's message." A prophet is a "proclaimer, one who speaks out the counsel of God with clearness, energy, and authority." In ancient days, prior to His completed revelation, God often used prophets or "proclaimers" to warn people about the future. Virtually all God wanted foretold, He ultimately inspired in His written

Word, the Bible. So the gift of prophecy is most often used today as the proclamation of God's truth. Whether or not they foretold any part of the future, Philip's four daughters—in today's terms—were Christian speakers!

Surrendering to His will doesn't mean you lose. Ultimately it means you win. One day you'll understand and see His glory.

In Acts 2:18 God said He would pour out His Spirit on both men and women. I believe the growing numbers of strong Christian men and women speakers are examples of God's fulfillment of His promise. I am convinced we are living in the midst of a significant work of God on His kingdom calendar.

Speaking of prophets, Paul encountered another at the house of Philip. His name was Agabus. And like Ezekiel of old, Agabus delivered his message through an enacted parable. By tying his own hands and feet, Agabus predicted that imprisonment awaited Paul in Jerusalem.

Agabus must have been extremely convincing because his actions had a far greater impact than the disciples' words in Tyre. On his last stop, although Luke and the others accompanied Paul to Tyre, only the Phoenician disciples urged him not to go to Jerusalem (see 21:4). In Caesarea, after Agabus's prophetic performance, Luke, the other missionaries, and the people *all* urged Paul not to go (see v. 12).

In turn, Paul also responded with strong emotion. Though he could hardly tear himself away from the Ephesian elders in Acts 20:37, he never wavered in his resolve. He also remained unmoved when the disciples in Tyre urged him not to go. Yet we see him respond with enormous emotion when his beloved associates—Luke, Timothy, and the others—wept and pleaded with him not to go. Let's try to capture an accurate picture. These men were not just crying. The original word for "weeping" is the strongest expression of grief in the Greek language. These men were sobbing. Paul responded tenderly, "What are you doing, weeping and breaking my heart?" (Acts 21:13).

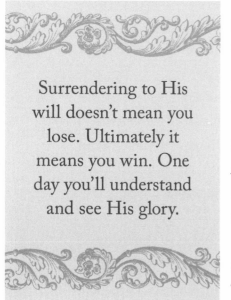

Paul's beloved friends were so crushed over what awaited him that their strength dissolved, their noble sense of purpose disintegrated, and they begged him not to go. Had he not been so convinced of the Spirit's compelling him to go, he surely would have changed his mind. He voiced his determination to each of them: "I am ready not only to be bound, but also to die in Jerusalem for the name of the Lord Jesus" (v. 13b).

We sometimes feel as if we're playing tug-of-war with God. In bitter tears we sometimes let go of the rope, tumble to the ground, and cry, "Have your way, God! You're going to do what You want anyway!" God is not playing a game. He doesn't jerk on the rope just so He can win. In fact, He doesn't want us to let go of the rope at all. Rather than see us drop the rope and give up, He wants us to hang on and let Him pull us over to His side.

God's will is always best even when we cannot imagine how. Surrendering to His will doesn't mean you lose. Ultimately it means you win. Keep hanging on to that rope and let Him pull you over to His side. One day you'll understand. And you'll see His glory.

What has been your most recent, most serious struggle with God? What do you suspect would happen if you totally submitted to His will and way?

Praying God's Word Today

You have made the contrast clear, Lord. Those whose lives are according to the flesh think about the things of the flesh, but those whose lives are according to the Spirit, about the things of the Spirit. The mind-set of the flesh is hostile to You because it does not submit itself to Your law, for it is unable to do so, unable to please You. We, however, are not in the flesh, but in the Spirit, since Your Spirit lives in us (Rom. 8:5, 7–9). May I want only what You know is best. May I not only let you have Your way with me but consider it a joy to follow You.

Day 53

Mixed Reviews

BEFORE YOU BEGIN

Read Acts 21:15–25

STOP AND CONSIDER

How many thousands of Jews there are who have believed. . . . But they have been told . . . that you teach all the Jews who are among the Gentiles to abandon Moses. (vv. 20–21)

What are some of the first things to go through your mind when your good intentions are going misunderstood? ____________________

____

____

When was the last time you were stuck in the middle of a situation involving Christians on both sides? What was the problem, and how did it work out?

____

____

____

Over the objections of the other believers, Paul set his face to go to Jerusalem. But if his arrival in Jerusalem had been a performance, he certainly would have received mixed reviews.

1. *Paul met acceptance.* What blessed words these are: "When we reached Jerusalem, the brothers welcomed us gladly" (v. 17). Don't miss Luke's terminology: "When *we* reached Jerusalem." After being unsuccessful in their attempt to plead with Paul to avoid going there, one would not be surprised if Paul's companions had said, "You go ahead if you want. The rest of us refuse to be so foolish."

Nearly thirty years earlier, Christ's disciples also tried to talk Him out of going back to Judea when they knew trouble awaited Him. When He could not be dissuaded, Thomas said, "Let's go so that we may die with Him" (John 11:16). Neither group was called to give their lives in association with their leader at this point, but surely God acknowledged their willingness.

What a sigh of relief must have come when Paul and his associates were greeted with warmth and approval by the believers in Jerusalem. Only one verse attests to Paul's testimony to James, the elders, and the others (Acts 21:19), but you can assume he talked for some time as "he related one by one what God did among the Gentiles through his ministry." The hearts of James and the others are evident in their reception of his testimony: "they glorified God" (v. 20). Notice, they did not praise Paul. Unfortunately acceptance was not the only response Paul met.

2. *Paul met apprehension.* After hearing Paul's wonderful news, James and the elders had good news of their own, and a little bad news. They gave Paul the good news first: "how many thousands of Jews there are who have believed" (v. 20). What glorious words! What could Paul have wanted more? According to Romans 9:3, absolutely nothing! He would have agreed to be cursed forever if the Jews would accept Christ. I wonder if Paul immediately began shouting hallelujah and dancing and praising God. Regardless, they jumped quickly to the bad news.

They almost seemed to be sparing his dignity. Yes, many had believed in Christ, but James and the elders observed, "All of them are zealous for the law. . . . But they have been informed that you . . . [tell] them not to live according to our customs" (vv. 20–21 NIV). In other words, they're saved—but they're mad. Talk about throwing a bucket of ice water on a warm reception.

Perhaps you know how Paul felt when he met disapproval among his own and found he had been misunderstood.

This dilemma draws compassion from my heart for both James and Paul. I feel compassion for James. We have all been in his position. He was caught in the middle of anger and disagreement between people he cared about. Just imagine the gnawing in James's stomach as Paul was giving a detailed account of all God was doing among the Gentiles. James knew he would have to tell Paul about the Jews.

I also feel compassion for Paul. He expected opposition from unbelievers, but to be hit immediately in Jerusalem by the disapproval of fellow believers must have drained his energy and excitement. Furthermore, much of what they were saying about him wasn't even accurate. He never told Jewish Christians not to circumcise their children. He told them not to insist that Gentile Christians circumcise theirs! He was trying to make the point that circumcision had nothing whatsoever to do with salvation.

Perhaps you know how Paul felt when he met disapproval among his own and found he had been misunderstood. Have you ever thought, "I expected this kind of thing from unbelievers, but I wasn't expecting this from my own fellow believers"? If so, you are part of a large fraternity, with Paul as a charter member.

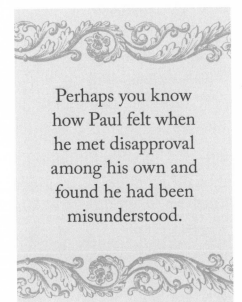

James and the elders immediately suggested that Paul join four men in their purification rites, so that all would see he still respected the customs. Paul submitted to their authority and did as they asked. His point regarding the ancient Hebrew customs was to practice them when wise or observe them as a reminder but not to live under them as a burden and a means of salvation.

Several times in Paul's ministry he was placed in a similar position with both Jews and Gentiles. He explained his actions in 1 Corinthians 9:19–23. He said that though he was free in Christ, he made himself a slave to everyone so that he could win as many as possible. He said he became like a Jew to the Jews in order to win the Jews, and like a Gentile to the Gentiles in order to win the Gentiles. Paul's great summary statement challenges every believer: "I have become all things to all people, so that I may by all means save some" (1 Cor. 9:22).

Like Paul, each of us must seek common ground with those who do not know Christ. We can respond legalistically and shun harmless practices, but if we do, we risk alienating the very people we want to reach.

How difficult is it for you to seek common ground with unbelievers without compromising Christian truth? What are the struggles inherent in this juggling act? Where do you locate the balancing point? ______________________________

PRAYING GOD'S WORD TODAY

Sometimes, Lord, it is not an enemy who insults me—otherwise I could bear it; it is not a foe who rises up against me—otherwise I could hide from him. But it is a man who is my peer, my companion and good friend! We used to have close fellowship; we walked with the crowd into the house of God. His buttery words are smooth, but war is in his heart. His words are softer than oil, but they are drawn swords. As for me, I will cast my burden on You, Lord, knowing that You will support me; You will never allow the righteous to be shaken (Ps. 55:12–14, 21–22). May I be true to You though others are false to me.

Day 54

Kill Him!

BEFORE YOU BEGIN

Read Acts 21:26–36

STOP AND CONSIDER

When Paul got to the steps, he had to be carried by the soldiers because of the mob's violence, for the mass of people were following and yelling, "Kill him!" (vv. 35–36)

How consistently do you keep up with the persecution of fellow believers in nations around the world? Why is it so important to pray for them? What difference does it make?

Have you stopped to ponder how you would react under life-threatening conditions, when one word of renouncement would get you off the hook? What makes endurance possible?

As we saw in yesterday's reading, Paul met welcome acceptance from some of the believers in Jerusalem. He met discouraging apprehension from others. Sadly, he also met a third reception: *accusation*. Imagine the moment. Paul and the Asian Jews, who had given him so much trouble in Ephesus, saw each other. I have a feeling Paul thought, "Oh, no!" and the Asian Jews thought, "Oh, yes!" They stirred up the crowd in the temple, the entire city fell into an uproar, and they grabbed Paul and tried to beat him to death. Can you imagine what the apostle was thinking? Surrounded by such a mob, I'm sure he thought he was about to draw his last breath. I can hardly imagine being beaten by *one* person. What would it be like to be beaten by a gang?

Did Paul recall the image of the prophet Agabus tied up with his belt? Paul had expected to be seized, but I'm not sure expectation and preparation are always synonymous. I don't think Paul was prepared for a mob to keep shouting, "Wipe this person off the earth—it's a disgrace for him to live!" (Acts 22:22). Was he ready for hatred and wholesale rejection by the people he would have given his life for? I'm not sure how adequately a person can prepare for such pain.

Later, in his letter to the Philippians (3:10), Paul made a reference to wanting the fellowship of sharing in Christ's sufferings. Paul received Christ by faith, knew Christ by name, but came face-to-face with Christ through experience. He spoke to Him through prayer. He grew in Him through the Word. But this particular day, Paul experienced a fellowship in His sufferings unlike any he had ever encountered.

Both Christ and Paul knew suffering was inevitable. Both Christ and Paul knew they would end up giving their lives—One as the Savior of the world, the other as His servant. Both grieved over Jerusalem. Both felt compelled to return to the holy city. Both knew the horror of being swept up in an angry mob. Both experienced the newness of every rejection. But no matter how many times it comes, one can hardly prepare for people who wish you dead. Paul did not know what would happen to him, but he did know Christ. As the apostle fellowshipped in His sufferings, he had never known Jesus better.

Praying God's Word Today

Lord, it encourages my heart to know this: as the sufferings of Christ overflow to me, so my comfort overflows through Christ. As I share in the sufferings, so I will share in the comfort (2 Cor. 1:5, 7). So even when I go through the darkest valley, I will fear no danger, for You are with me; Your rod and Your staff—they comfort me (Ps. 23:4).

Day 55

Salvation Story

Before You Begin

Read Acts 22:1–21

Stop and Consider

"Brothers and fathers, listen now to my defense before you." When they heard that he was addressing them in the Hebrew language, they became even quieter. (vv. 1–2)

What has always struck you as the most intriguing parts of Paul's conversion? Which ones fire your imagination and excitement? Which make the richest doctrinal statements?

How do you rate your own salvation story? How many times have you told it to someone? What could inspire you to tell it again?

Acts 22 contains Paul's account of his own Damascus-road conversion. His approach contains several elements that build a powerful testimony. We can learn from the following four elements in sharing our own testimonies.

1. *Paul communicated simply and clearly.* Paul spoke in Greek to the commander and in Aramaic to the Jews. Few of us are fluent in several languages, as Paul was, but we can apply his example, learning to communicate more effectively by speaking the language of our hearers.

I grew up going to Sunday school and church. I spent much of my early social life with other Christians, so I had a difficult time learning to speak a language an unchurched person could understand. My speech was so laced and interwoven with church terms that those unacquainted with church life could hardly understand me. I practically needed an interpreter!

I still have to remind myself to resist assuming every listener knows the lingo. I'm learning to use figures of speech and expressions that lost people will more likely understand. I'm also, like, you know, learning to use more contemporary expressions when speaking to youth. Of course, learning to speak understandably does not mean adopting any level of vulgarity. It means speaking with a greater level of clarity.

2. *Paul honestly described his former conduct.* We lose our listeners the moment they sense an attitude of superiority in us. Paul spoke with honesty and humility. As he explained his background and his persecutions of the church, he related with them as one who had been exactly where they were. Not all of us have a background as dramatically different from our present lifestyles as Paul did, yet we have all been lost. Lost is lost.

Remember an important principle about sharing our former conduct. Generalizations usually are best. I try to avoid becoming specific about ungodly actions in my past. I want the listener to focus on my Savior, not my behavior. Sometimes we glorify ungodly behavior by highlighting how bad we were. This method can dishonor God, and it can dishonor the listener by stirring unnecessary mental images of sin. Share past conduct with caution!

3. *Paul related his experience of conversion.* Few of us have experienced the dramatic conversion Paul described in Acts 22:6–16, but we can tell how we accepted Christ. Don't think your testimony is meaningless if you didn't have a dramatic conversion. Every conversion cost the same amount of Christ's blood shed on the cross. Yours is just as meaningful as the most dramatic conversion ever told.

Every conversion cost the same amount of Christ's blood. Yours is just as meaningful as the most dramatic conversion ever told.

In the parable of the prodigal son, the elder brother felt insulted because the father accepted his brother after a season of wild living (Luke 15:29–30). He didn't understand the biggest difference between the two brothers was that the prodigal son had to live with the personal loss and suffering. If your conversion was less sensational than others, praise God for less drama! With it probably came less pain! You don't have to see a bright light from heaven to have a story to tell. The determining factor is not how exciting your conversion was but how excited you are now about your conversion.

4. *Paul shared how he received his commission.* He was very clear that God had a purpose for his life. The people we talk to need to know that there is life after salvation! Salvation is not only about eternity. Salvation is also the open door to a rich earthly life in which we enjoy the love and direction of an active God.

Many unbelievers are repelled by Christianity because they are afraid they'll have to give up so much in order to live for Christ. As we share our testimonies, we can help them see all we've gained since Jesus came into our hearts, all the ways our lives have been blessed and enhanced by His presence within us. Make your sense of ongoing purpose a part of your testimony. We often have no idea how much people are struggling to find a reason to live and to persevere through difficulty.

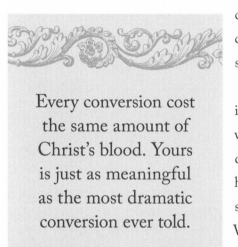

This seemed like a good place to jot down some notes on your own salvation story, using the rough outline provided by the four theme's in today's reading. Enjoy remembering . . .

PRAYING GOD'S WORD TODAY

Father God, You have given me a marvelous story to tell—how You have rescued me from the domain of darkness and transferred me into the kingdom of Your beloved Son, in whom I have redemption, the forgiveness of sins (Col. 1:13–14). I have been crucified with Christ; and I no longer live, but Christ lives in me. The life I now live in the flesh, I live by faith in Your Son, who loved me and gave Himself for me (Gal 2:19–20). May I not hide this from my children but tell a future generation Your praises, Your might, and the wonderful works You have performed, so that a future generation—children yet to be born—might know. Then they will rise and tell their children so they might put their confidence in You, not forget Your works, but keep Your commandments (Ps. 78:4, 6–7). This is my prayer. Show me fresh, new ways and opportunities to tell my story.

Day 56

Unseen Success

BEFORE YOU BEGIN

Read Acts 22:22–29

STOP AND CONSIDER

The commander ordered him to be brought into the barracks, directing that he be examined with the scourge, so he could discover the reason they were shouting. (v. 24)

Think of someone (or perhaps several someones) whose salvation has been the cry of your heart for a long time? How does their continued refusal to receive Christ affect you?

How do you personally judge the success of any undertaking—spiritual or otherwise? Why are end results so often a poor judge of that?

On a human scale we cannot judge Paul's visit to Jerusalem a success. Perhaps his experiences in places like Athens and Jerusalem will teach us to think differently about success and failure. Hopefully we will come to understand that in our Christian lives, success is obedience to God, not results we can measure.

I'm sure Paul wanted to bear fruit in Jerusalem more than any place on earth. Yet we see him face greater opposition and struggle in Jerusalem than virtually anywhere in his ministry. In the holy city Paul was forced to measure his ministry strictly on his obedience to the Spirit, not outward results.

Unfortunately the Jews didn't think much of Paul's purpose on this earth. Once he acknowledged the importance of the Gentiles to God, he lost his audience. Sadly their personal need to feel superior exceeded their spiritual sensibilities.

Paul desperately wanted the Jews to receive Christ. Was he a failure because they rejected him? Was his testimony shared in vain? Absolutely not. God had compelled Paul to go to Jerusalem. He had warned him of hardships. He had given Paul an opportunity to share his testimony with the very people who had just tried to kill him.

Did they hear Paul's message? Oh, yes. Otherwise, they would not have responded so emotionally. Few of those in hearing distance that day forgot Paul's testimony. We cannot judge effectiveness from immediate results. According to John 14:26, the Holy Spirit can remind a person of truth taught long ago. When we obey God, we find great comfort in leaving the consequences up to Him.

Paul avoided a flogging because God equipped him with Roman citizenship even before his birth. God used every ounce and detail of Paul's past, even his unique citizenship. I want God to use every ounce of me too. Paul poured himself out like a drink offering in Jerusalem. He received little encouragement to preach while he was there—but he continued. Paul's certainty of what he had been called to do was exceeded only by his certainty of who called. Paul considered Him who called worth it all.

Praying God's Word Today

You reign, Lord! The world is firmly established; it cannot be shaken. You judge the peoples fairly. So let the heavens be glad and the earth rejoice; let the sea and all that fills it resound. Let the fields and everything in them exult. Then all the trees of the forest will shout for joy before You, for You are coming—coming to judge the earth. You will judge the world with righteousness and the peoples with Your faithfulness (Ps. 96:10–13). I put my trust and reputation in Your strong hands, Lord, for You will make all things known.

Day 57

Conscious of Conscience

Before You Begin

Read Acts 22:30–23:1

Stop and Consider

Paul looked intently at the Sanhedrin and said, "Brothers, I have lived my life before God in all good conscience until this day." (v. 1)

What kind of terms have you and your conscience been on lately? If you had to describe your relationship with your conscience, how would you put it into words?

How have you grown more sensitive to the voice of conscience? Would you say you're becoming more quickly aware of its first signs of discomfort? If so, or if not—why?

We learn volumes about Paul by noting his priorities. A clear conscience was no doubt one of them, since he spoke of it often in his letters. The Greek word for "conscience" is *suneidesis*, which means "to be one's own witness, one's own conscience coming forward as a witness. It denotes an abiding consciousness whose nature it is to bear witness to one's own conduct in a moral sense. It is self-awareness." In lay terms we might say the conscience is an inner constituent casting a vote about the rightness of our behaviors.

God's Word helps us compile several facts concerning the conscience:

1. *People without a spotless past can enjoy a clear conscience.* What wonderful news! Paul spoke of possessing a clear conscience numerous times, yet he considered himself one of the worst possible offenders. His conscience was clear even though he had wronged many people in the past. A clear conscience is possible for those of us who have sinned.

2. *Good deeds cannot accomplish a clear conscience.* Have you ever tried to worship or serve God when your conscience was bothering you after an unsettled argument with your spouse or a coworker? Or perhaps after telling a lie to someone? Hebrews 9:9 tells us of two things that will never clear the conscience of the worshipper: gifts and sacrifices. We've all probably tried to soothe our consciences with good works. God's Word tells us we cannot offer enough gifts or sacrifices to clear a guilty conscience. Take heart! The Bible does give us some steps to a clear conscience.

3. *The Holy Spirit works with the believer's conscience.* The Holy Spirit plays a critical role in creating and maintaining a clear conscience. In Romans 9:1, Paul said the Holy Spirit confirmed his conscience. Once we have received Christ and the Holy Spirit resides within us, the Holy Spirit will work with our consciences. The Spirit works both to confirm a clear conscience and to convict a guilty conscience. We all naturally prefer to ignore our sin. The one part of us that does not ignore sin is our conscience. For that reason the Holy Spirit deals with conscience first, not with our intellect or emotions. You might think of the relationship this way: the Holy Spirit plants conviction in the soil of the conscience. If ignored, that conviction will usually grow and grow.

4. *The conscience is an indicator, not a transformer.* Only the Holy Spirit can change us and clear our consciences. By itself, all the conscience can do with a guilty person is condemn. My conscience may lend an awareness of what I ought to do, but it supplies little power to do it. The believer possesses something far greater. The Holy Spirit who resides in us supplies abundant power not only to recognize the right thing, but to do it!

Can we really have clear consciences? The Bible says we can. Considering Paul's past, if he can have a clear conscience, any of us can. Like me, you may have discovered that asking God for forgiveness doesn't always make you feel better. Sometimes we know we're forgiven, but we still feel a load of guilt. How can we discover the freedom of a clear conscience? I believe Hebrews 10:22 holds several vital keys: "Let us draw near with a true heart in full assurance of faith, our hearts sprinkled clean from an evil conscience and our bodies washed in pure water." Consider these steps to a clear conscience:

Can we really have clear consciences? Considering Paul's past, if he can have a clear conscience, any of us can.

Bring your heavy conscience to God. When we have a guilty conscience, we shy away from the presence of God. We tend to resist what we need most: an awareness of God's love! Draw near to God!

Approach God with absolute sincerity. Come entirely clean before Him. Spill your heart and confess everything you feel. Tell Him about the guilt that continues to nag at you. You'll not only clear your heart and mind, you'll tattle on the evil one who has no right to keep accusing you after repentance.

Ask God to give you full assurance of His love and acceptance. In His Word, God tells you over and over how much He loves you. He assures you of His forgiveness. He also tells you He forgets your confessed sin. Ask God to give you faith to take Him at His Word. You needn't fear rejection or ridicule. Let Him reassure you of His love and forgiveness.

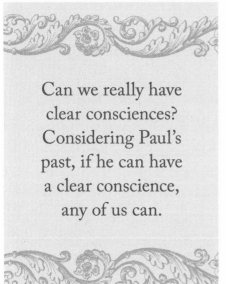

Picture the cross of Christ once more. Really take a good mental look at it. Was Christ's death on the cross enough to cover your sin? Enough to take away your guilt? Yes. He gave everything He had for everything we've said, done, or thought. Then picture yourself at the foot of His cross, close enough to have your heart cleansed by His redemptive blood. No sin is too grievous. No load is too heavy for Christ to carry. Walk away free, and leave with God that old condemning tape you've been playing over and over on your mental "recorder"!

Like the apostle Paul, we can enjoy a clear conscience even after a guilty past. Don't wait another moment. "Draw near to God" (Heb. 10:22 NIV).

Paul spoke about having a clear conscience "toward God and men" (Acts 24:16). How should you handle a situation in which you've sinned against both? If an instance comes to mind, what are you going to do to make amends and, if possible, restore relationship?

PRAYING GOD'S WORD TODAY

Lord Jesus, You have told us that if we are offering our gift on the altar, and there we remember that our brother (or sister) has something against us, we should leave our gift there in front of the altar. We must first go and be reconciled with our brother, and then come and offer our gift (Matt. 5:23–24). May You give me the courage, the words, and the initiative to be obedient to You in this matter. I want my conscience clear at all costs.

Day 58

Anger Management

Before You Begin

Read Acts 23:2–10

Stop and Consider

"God is going to strike you, you whitewashed wall! You are sitting there judging me according to the law, and in violation of the law are you ordering me to be struck?" (v. 3)

Have you noticed an occasional tendency to adopt our foe's tactics—like, if they lose control of their mouths, sometimes we follow suit? Has anything like that happened lately?

Where does anger rate on your list of personal problem areas? What have you learned about yourself in dealing with it? How is anger a help, and how is anger a hurt?

During his stay in Jerusalem, Paul had no need to make a living. God had already booked him a room in the city jail. God did not allow the apostle to be jailed to his harm but to provide a means of safety for him while allowing him to share his testimony in the highest courts, as in the case of Acts 23 and his appearance before the Sanhedrin and Ananias, the high priest.

Why was Ananias so insulted at Paul's confession about living before God "in all good conscience" (Acts 23:1)—insulted enough to have Paul struck in the mouth? Was it because Paul referred to them as "brothers"? Or could it have been because Paul was indirectly suggesting a conscience check for everyone listening?

Unfortunately we don't have the benefit of hearing Paul's voice inflection. But his response instantly following the slap suggests he might have been ready for an altercation. "God is going to strike you, you whitewashed wall!" (v. 3). I'm quite sure the temperature in the room rose dramatically. After Paul called Ananias a name, those standing close to him said, "Do you dare revile God's high priest?" (v. 4). Don't miss Paul's response. "I did not know, brothers, that it was the high priest" (v. 5).

If we could have heard Paul's voice, I believe his inflection might have contained a little sarcasm. No doubt Paul knew he was insulting the high priest. He was far too knowledgeable not to have recognized Ananias's robes and obvious position of honor. I believe he knew he was insulting the high priest and probably offended him further by saying, in effect, "Sorry, but I never would have recognized this guy as a high priest."

I'm suggesting Paul may have been in an interesting mood, and if I may be so bold, even a touch of an insolent mood. I mean absolutely no disrespect to the apostle, but I believe he sometimes struggled with a temper. And when dealing with a foe like Ananias, whom history records as a very insolent, hot-tempered man, the sight of his false piety and that of the other religious leaders probably made Paul's stomach turn—especially because he had been one of them. Sometimes the ugliest picture we see of ourselves is the one we see in others. And even a great man like Paul can find it to be more than he can take.

Praying God's Word Today

Grow in me the patience, Lord, to live by these words of Yours: "Commit your way to the Lord; trust in Him, and He will act, making your righteousness shine like the dawn, your justice like the noonday. Be silent before the Lord and wait expectantly for Him; do not be agitated by one who prospers in his way, by the man who carries out evil plans. Refrain from anger and give up your rage; do not be agitated—it can only bring harm. For evildoers will be destroyed, but those who put their hope in the Lord will inherit the land" (Ps. 37:5–9). I know this in my head. May I live it in my heart and life.

Day 59

Courage!

Before You Begin

Read Acts 23:11–22

Stop and Consider

The following night, the Lord stood by him and said, "Have courage! For as you have testified about Me in Jerusalem, so you must also testify in Rome." (v. 11)

How desperate is your need for courage right now? What are you facing that cannot be dealt with by anything less than God's gift of holy grit and determination?

How have you experienced a transfer of courage from God before? To what could you testify about the Lord's faithfulness to supply His people strength when needed?

Sometimes we must read between the lines in the book of Acts to see Paul the man and not just his travels. Acts 23:11 offers us a perfect opportunity to read between the lines without stretching the text. I hope Christ's tenderness toward His willing captive touches you. He stood near Paul and said, "Have courage!"

Why did Christ draw so physically close to Paul at this particular moment? I believe Paul was overcome with fear and may have been convinced he would not live much longer. He had looked straight into the eyes of rage. He was separated from his friends. He was imprisoned by strangers. I believe he was terrified.

Later Paul wrote from another prison cell, "My God will supply all your needs according to His riches in glory in Christ Jesus" (Phil. 4:19). He could make such a claim because God had been so faithful to meet his needs. In Acts 23:11 God looked on His servant Paul imprisoned in Jerusalem, and He didn't just see emotions. He saw the need they represented. Paul was afraid. He needed courage. Just like Philippians 4:19 said, God literally met his need in Christ Jesus. That day in Paul's prison cell, Christ stood near and said, "Have courage!" He meant, "I'm right here. Take courage from Me!"

The Lord gave Paul great motivation for courage by giving him confirmation: Paul was going to Rome. His life could not be taken until the mission was complete. Paul surely knew that Christ's confirmation did not mean Paul wouldn't suffer or be greatly persecuted. He simply knew he could not be killed until he had testified about Christ in Rome.

God timed Paul's injection of courage perfectly to offset the conspiracy to kill Paul. Overnight in Jerusalem Paul became the center of a dangerous whirlwind of rage that rapidly gained force. By morning, forty men bound themselves with an oath to kill him. The original terminology tells us they were binding themselves to a curse if they didn't carry out their plans. They may not have realized they had bound themselves to a curse already! In the words of Micah the prophet: "Woe to those who dream up wickedness and prepare evil plans on their beds! . . . Therefore, the Lord says: 'I am now planning disaster against this nation; you cannot free your necks from it'" (Mic. 2:1, 3).

Praying God's Word Today

Sometimes I must confess with David that troubles without number have surrounded me; my sins have overtaken me; I am unable to see. They are more than the hairs of my head, and my courage leaves me. But Lord, be pleased to deliver me; hurry to help me. For I know that those who seek You rejoice and are glad in You. Those who love Your salvation continually say, "The Lord is great!" I am afflicted and needy, Father, and yet You think of me. You are my help and my deliverer. O God, do not delay! (Ps. 40:12–13, 16–17).

Day 60

Delivered Royally

BEFORE YOU BEGIN

Read Acts 23:23–35

STOP AND CONSIDER

"Get 200 soldiers ready with 70 cavalry and 200 spearmen to go to Caesarea at nine tonight. Also provide mounts so they can put Paul on them." (vv. 23–24)

Sometimes God delivers us *from* peril, and sometimes He delivers us *through* peril. How have you experienced both? ______________________________

____

____

What goes through your mind when you see God sweeping the prisoner Paul to safety under a whole detachment of Roman guards? What must his conspirators have thought?

____

____

____

We have already had a number of occasions to consider God's creativity in terms of His methods of delivery. He can shake the foundations of a prison, or He can employ the Roman cavalry to accompany a servant out of town. But note one constant that Paul addressed in his second letter to the Corinthians: "We have placed our hope in Him that He will deliver us again. And you can join in helping with prayer for us" (2 Cor. 1:10–11). Never underestimate the effects of intercessory prayer lifted for our deliverance. Never underestimate the effects of your prayers for others.

The year I began working on this study of Paul, my heart was torn to pieces over a devastating loss. For several months no one outside our family and friends knew about it. Because the wound was so fresh, we were not yet able to tell the story. Letters poured in from all over the nation saying something like this: "God has placed a heavy burden on my heart for Beth and her family. I do not know what is wrong, but I'm praying for them." I could hardly believe it. Once we shared more openly about our loss, we learned that literally thousands of people were praying for us. I am absolutely certain those prayers delivered us from the pit of despair. Many times my soul would sink in grief. I'd feel like I was about to descend into depression. But each time I began to slip, I sensed something like a supernatural net disallowing me to descend another inch.

God can deliver anyone from anything at any time. He doesn't need any help. Yet He invites us to be part of His great work through prayer. If we don't intercede for one another, we miss opportunities to see His deliverance and thank Him for His faithfulness. I like to call this God's profit-sharing plan. When we pray for one another, we share the blessings when deliverance comes because we've been personally involved. Their thanksgiving becomes our thanksgiving.

Many scholars believe Paul wrote 2 Corinthians on his third missionary journey, prior to his arrest in Jerusalem. If so, the Corinthians' prayers were actively involved in Paul's deliverance. He rode in style to Caesarea, surrounded by soldiers, horsemen, spearmen, and the prayers of the Corinthian Christians.

Praying God's Word Today

Lord God, my strong Savior, You shield my head on the day of battle (Ps. 140:7) through the prayers of Your people and the help that comes from the Spirit of Christ (Phil. 1:19). How encouraging to know that our prayers don't just vanish into thin air but, like smoke rising from incense, the prayers of the saints come up into Your presence (Rev. 8:4). Thank You for hearing us—and acting—as we pray for one another, even today, even right now.

Day 61

Personally Speaking

Before You Begin

Read Acts 24:22–27

Stop and Consider

As [Paul] spoke about righteousness, self-control, and the judgment to come, Felix became afraid and replied, "Leave for now, but when I find time I'll call for you." (v. 25)

Why do you think God is willing to go to such great lengths to have His gospel proclaimed to those who have no interest in receiving it? ____________________

Perhaps you, too, know someone who is waiting for a later time before they seriously consider the claims of Christ. What do you think they're really waiting for?

As we begin today's reading, my mind drifts back over the many stops we've made with the apostle Paul. I suppose none of us wants to trade times, places, and lives with him; but each of us must admit that Paul's tenure on this earth was extremely fascinating. He could write about "the breadth, and length, and depth, and height" (Eph. 3:18 KJV) because he experienced each of those extremes. This man we're studying in God's Word was flesh and blood. But he was extraordinary.

Acts 24 unfolds with Paul incarcerated in Caesarea after being escorted by a grand cavalry. Ananias the high priest arrived with an entourage, including a lawyer named Tertullus who brought the charges against Paul before the governor. Few things are more disgusting than a political spiel that bears no resemblance to the truth. Tertullus began by flattering Felix, the governor. Judging by the lawyer's words, Felix deserved his own holiday for being a peacemaker, a reformer, a tireless officer, and a noble man! Tertullus knew better. Felix was vile and incompetent. Nero had him recalled only two years later. He was a former slave who had cunningly gained favor with the imperial court, "known for his violent use of repressive force and corrupt self-aggrandizement."[13]

After blatantly flattering Felix, Tertullus delivered his charges against Paul. He said that Paul was a troublemaker who stirred up riots among the Jews and that he had tried to desecrate the temple (see vv. 5–8). Paul responded to the charges with a forthright description of his journey to Jerusalem and the events there.

Felix obviously viewed the conflict as a no-win situation. The size of the Jewish community and the Roman citizenship of Paul left Felix in a dilemma. He lacked the wisdom to make an appropriate decision, so he did nothing. He left Paul in prison. God, however, was clearly up to something. Several days after the hearing, God gave Paul an interesting opportunity. He sent the preacher to a congregation of two: Felix and Drusilla. Drusilla was the third wife of the governor, and both of them had deserted previous spouses to marry. God equipped Paul with a tailor-made lesson for the two. Verse 25 tells us Paul "discoursed," which means "to speak back and forth or alternately, to converse with."

He didn't just give a sermon. He led Felix and Drusilla in an interactive study. The core of Paul's message was "faith in Christ Jesus" (v. 24).

The apostle's message contained three points: "righteousness, self-control and the judgment to come." We could summarize his message like this: salvation by grace teaches us to live self-controlled lives. Paul risked bodily harm when he preached such a forceful message to Governor Felix and his wife. Christ had assured the apostle he would go to Rome, so he knew he wouldn't be killed; but torture can be a more difficult prospect than death! You can be sure Paul didn't bring the message Felix was expecting. He and Drusilla, a Jewess, most likely expected a message of mystical divinity. Instead they got a message of practical clarity, and every point stuck.

> Confrontation with personal sin is never convenient. Some of the messages I've needed to hear most, I wanted to hear least.

Felix was not amused by the outspoken preacher. Verse 25 tells us he "was afraid and said, 'That's enough for now! You may leave'" (NIV). I see some irony in his choice of words. History describes him as a man with a gross lack of self-control.[14] I have a feeling he rarely applied the words "That's enough for now" to himself. Felix told Paul he would send for him at a more convenient time.

I'm not sure confrontation with personal sin is ever convenient. Some of the messages I've needed to hear most were those I wanted to hear least. Like Felix, we in our human natures often resist what is best for us. But unlike Felix, we can dare to accept a truth and find freedom.

While Felix felt fear, Luke tells us of no reaction from Drusilla. We might surmise she was also convicted and frightened, but Scripture only tells us Felix was afraid. I would like to offer a different theory. Perhaps Drusilla simply did not humble herself enough to be afraid. She had quite an interesting heritage—one plagued with pride.

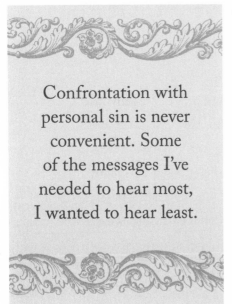

Remember Herod Agrippa I from Acts 12:19–23? He was Drusilla's father. He bestowed on himself the glory due only to God. As a result he was eaten by worms and then died. You might think having a father who was eaten alive by worms would have some impact. Instead, Drusilla led an adulterous life in spite of all she knew about morality and reverence for God from her Jewish heritage. The generational bondage of pride could have been broken with her father's dreadful demise. Instead she resisted the message, willingly picked up the chain of pride, and carried on.

God in His mercy reaches out to the immoral, ill-tempered, and boastful. Many hear but run the other way. Others hear but never apply. But some listen and are set free. God not only sent Felix and Drusilla a fitting message, He sent them a fitting messenger. Paul could not stand before them as one who had never experienced a terrible lack of self-control. He was once puffed with pride. His only righteousness was in the law. Then one day Jesus confronted him in the middle of his sin. He'd been running straight to Him ever since.

What kind of message might God be trying to get through to you right now, but you're putting off His warning, plugging your ears to His Word? What are you waiting for?

Praying God's Word Today

Lord, I am so grateful—and awed—that You do not delay Your promise, as some understand delay, but rather You are patient with us, not wanting any to perish, but all to come to repentance (2 Pet. 3:9), to be saved, to come to the knowledge of the truth (1 Tim. 2:4). May many understand today—especially those that I know and care about—that now is the acceptable time; look, now is the day of salvation (2 Cor. 6:2).

Day 62

Do You Hear What I Hear?

BEFORE YOU BEGIN

Read Acts 25:13–22

STOP AND CONSIDER

Agrippa said to Festus, "I would like to hear the man myself."
"Tomorrow," he said, "you will hear him." (v. 22)

If someone asked to hear your best defense of the gospel and of Christ's impact on your life, what are some of the things you would point to?

What are the main differences in believing something and knowing something? How has Christ become a "known" reality to you?

Acts 25 begins with the arrival of a new leader of the province. Festus replaced Felix, but Paul remained in prison. The Jewish leaders immediately appealed to the new governor to have Paul returned to Jerusalem for trial. Though two years had passed, and they were either very hungry or had abandoned their vow not to eat until Paul was dead, they still harbored such hatred of the apostle that they could think only of killing him. Rather than be returned to Jerusalem, Paul appealed to Caesar. Why he did remains a mystery.

After Festus heard Paul's defense, he said in effect, "I would turn him loose, but since he appealed to Caesar, I send him to Rome as a prisoner." We cannot judge from the words of Festus whether Paul might have been freed. What we do know is that the apostle is about to travel to Rome at last, but first he has one more chance to present the gospel.

King Agrippa and his wife Bernice came to Caesarea to pay respects to the new governor. Festus told them about Paul, and they decided to hear from the apostle. As Paul had done with Felix and Drusilla, he preached to the new trio. Festus's response contains a fascinating statement. He "was at a loss how to investigate" Paul's claims that a dead man named Jesus was alive (Acts 25:20 NIV).

I remember sharing with a loved one how I know Christ is alive. He said, "I believe in reincarnation," and, "I believe a spiritual presence exists rather than a certain God." He continued by repeating the words "I believe" over and over. Suddenly God gave me such a strange insight, and I was overwhelmed at the difference between my loved one and me. He believed the things he had been taught through New Age philosophy. I didn't just believe. *I knew.* I gently said to him, "My God is not just Someone I believe in. He's Someone I know. I've felt His presence. I've seen His activity. I've experienced His deliverance. I've been touched by His healing. I've witnessed answered prayer. I've 'heard' Him speak straight to me through His Word. Yes, I believe. But more than that, I know."

My loved one said nothing more, but I knew he heard my heart. Dead prophets simply don't save, guide, heal, deliver, answer prayers, or speak through an ancient text with the relevance of this morning's newspaper.

Praying God's Word Today

Thank You, Father, for the gift of Your precious Word, for writing these things to us who believe in the name of Your Son, so that we may know—may know!—that we have eternal life (1 John 5:13). We know, Lord, that the Son of God has come and has given us understanding so that we may know the true One. We are in the true One—that is, in His Son Jesus Christ. He is the true God and eternal life (1 John 5:20).

Day 63

Who, What, Where, When, How

Before You Begin

Read Acts 26:24–32

Stop and Consider

"King Agrippa, do you believe the prophets? I know you believe." Then Agrippa said to Paul, "Are you going to persuade me to become a Christian so easily?" (vv. 27–28)

What is something you're absolutely counting on from God right now—you're just not sure when it's going to happen? ______

______

______

How do we tend to put God in a box, only expecting Him to answer our prayers in certain ways, not really watching for any less predictable ones? ______

______

______

______

My advice to anyone who is investigating the matter of Christ's existence would probably be these two suggestions:

1. Open your heart to the possibility of Christ's authenticity by coming to church and getting to know Christian people.
2. Ask Christ if He's real, then be honest and open enough to watch for Him to reveal Himself.

Good investigators ask certain questions: who? what? where? when? how? The context of Acts 26 shows what we may know: who is in control and even what He's doing and where He's leading—but we'll rarely guess when and how! Let's take the Jewish leaders and Paul as an example of our inability to know these things.

1. *Neither Paul nor the Jewish leaders understood when.* Paul didn't know when God would fulfill His promise. Paul knew who had called him and what Christ had called him to do. He even knew where: God was going to send him to Rome. But Paul might never have guessed he would still be sitting in jail two years after the promise. That's why he probably asked God many times—When? Time means so much to you and me. When God sheds light on ministries He wants us to fulfill or promises He plans to keep, we usually assume He means right now! A study of the Jewish patriarchs, however, proves that years may separate God's promise and its fulfillment. Not one minute is wasted, but God rarely seems to fulfill His revealed plan when we expect.

Likewise, the Jews didn't know when God would fulfill His promise. They believed God would send the Messiah. That was the answer to who. They also knew what He would come to do: bring salvation. They were certain where: Israel, then to all parts of the world. But they didn't understand when. They were still looking for a Messiah, even though He had already come. Sometimes we can keep asking when God is going to do something He's already done!

2. *Neither Paul nor the Jewish leaders understood how.* God had assured Paul He was sending him to Rome, but Paul would never have guessed how. In Acts 25:25 Festus announced, "When he himself appealed to the Emperor, I decided to send him." Actually it was God who had decided to send Paul to Rome, but He was about to use Festus as the vehicle. Paul may have wondered over and over how he would ever get to Rome while under arrest. He probably asked his associates many times to pray for his release so he could fulfill his calling in Rome. I wonder if Paul ever imagined his arrest would be the tool God would use to give him an all-expenses paid trip to his destination.

When we don't know what, when, where, or how, we can trust in who. We won't always find our answers, but we can find our God.

I recently heard a famous actor share his testimony before a secular audience. He said when he was a boy, God revealed to him that he would reach out to thousands and thousands of people. All his life he had waited for God to call him to preach. God never did. Instead the young man developed into an Academy Award–winning actor. He was thankful for his opportunities to act, but he could not understand what had happened to his calling. The evening he was honored, he said he realized God had fulfilled His promise. The young boy never would have guessed how God would do what He said.

God is the Deliverer, but we never know how He might deliver us. We see that God always fulfills His promises, just not always the way we imagine.

If Paul was occasionally shocked by how God fulfilled His promises, he was not the only one. God had assured the Jews He would send the Messiah, but they never would have guessed how. They were expecting great pomp to accompany their king's arrival. They were not expecting someone who looked so ordinary, so common. They unfortunately wanted a prestigious king more than a servant Savior.

Praise God, He gives us what we need, not what we want. If Christ had come to immediately wear His crown, we would be hopelessly lost. A crown of thorns and a splintered cross had to precede a crown of jewels and a hallowed throne. If they hadn't, Christ would still have a throne but no earthly subjects to approach it.

God calls us to be good investigators. We don't have to be at a loss on how to investigate such matters. When we don't know what, when, where, or how, we can trust in who. We won't always find our answers, but we can always find our God when we seek Him with all our hearts. And He will love and comfort us until all other answers come.

What keeps you going in the midst of questions and unanswered situations? How do you typically deal with things you don't know and can't figure out?

Praying God's Word Today

Lord, may it be said of me that my heart is not proud; my eyes are not haughty. I do not get involved with things too great or too difficult for me. Instead, I have calmed and quieted myself like a little weaned child with its mother; I am like a little child, putting my hope in You, both now and forever (Ps. 131:1–3). For I know that You, Lord, are the God of all flesh. Is anything too difficult for You? (Jer. 32:27). Of course not. I trust You wholeheartedly.

Day 64

All Their Fault

Before You Begin

Read Acts 27:9–12

Stop and Consider

But the centurion paid attention to the captain
and the owner of the ship rather than to what Paul said. (v. 11)

Perhaps you're dealing with an issue right now where you can't get others to cooperate or agree with your advice and suggestions. How does this have you feeling and responding?

How have you been harmed by another person's errors, whether deliberate or accidental? What has this done to your relationship? How are you handling your anger or regret?

We ordinarily think of the apostle Paul as deeply spiritual, but Acts 27 reminds us he also could be rather practical. He had spent much time on ships traveling the Mediterranean. Winter was approaching. In ancient days few vessels risked the sea during the winter months.

Although Paul was no expert seaman, he also wasn't a man to keep his opinion to himself. He warned the pilot, the centurion, and the ship's owner, "Men, I can see that this voyage is headed toward damage and heavy loss" (Acts 27:10). Can you picture this little bearded man licking the end of his index finger and holding it up to check the direction of the wind? Paul might have been perceived as a know-it-all at times. This was one of those times when someone probably should have listened.

The pilot and owner insisted on sailing regardless of difficulty. Like a plot from a disaster movie, they put profit above safety. They let their ledgers eclipse their good sense. The Alexandrian ship serviced Rome with expensive grain. They took advantage of the first gentle breeze and headed out, running a risk that would eventually catch them right between the eyes, driving them helter-skelter on the open seas.

This particular peril in the apostle's life struck a chord in my heart for reasons I couldn't quite identify at first. I finally realized why: he and the others met great difficulty because of someone else's poor judgment.

I've gone through storms as a direct result of my own rebellion. I've also gone through storms as a result of spiritual warfare. Others were ordained directly by God for His glory. But sometimes the most difficult storms of all can be those that result from another person's poor judgment. A wrong decision by a business partner, a boss, a driver, a jury, a teacher, a child, or a spouse can have devastating repercussions on other lives.

Of the four origins of personal storms I just identified, the one caused by someone else's poor judgment has its own unique difficulty because we have someone else in flesh and blood to blame! We feel much greater potential for bitterness and unforgiveness. If you find yourself in that position, keep your eyes (as Paul did) on God's greater purpose.

Praying God's Word Today

Lord, I seek refuge in You; never let me be disgraced. In Your justice, rescue and deliver me; listen closely to me and save me. Be a rock of refuge for me, where I can always go. Give the command to save me, for You are my rock and fortress. Deliver me, my God, from the hand of the wicked, from the grasp of the unjust and oppressive. For You are my hope, Lord God, my confidence from my youth. I have leaned on You from birth; You took me from my mother's womb. My praise is always about You. I have become an ominous sign to many, but You are my strong refuge. My mouth is full of praise and honor to You all day long (Ps. 71:1–8).

Day 65

Weathering the Storm

Before You Begin

Read Acts 27:13–26

Stop and Consider

For many days neither sun nor stars appeared, and the severe storm kept raging; finally all hope that we would be saved was disappearing. (v. 20)

What are some of the things you've learned from your own experiences when "neither sun nor stars appeared, and the severe storm kept raging"?

The crew in charge of Paul's ship eventually started throwing some things overboard to lighten their load. Are you carrying any extra baggage you should probably do without?

The sailors on board with Paul took steps to deal with the storm that enveloped their ship. In their actions I see practical behaviors we can also apply in our lives for surviving our personal storms. Although the points I am about to make might not apply to a literal ship on an angry sea, they will be helpful in the storms we encounter when someone close to us exercises poor judgment.

1. *Don't pull up the anchor* (see v. 13). The ship's masters were ill advised to attempt to sail, but they decided to weigh anchor anyway. Jesus Christ is our anchor beyond the veil (see Heb. 6:19–20). When gentle breezes blow in our lives and all seems calm and peaceful, we often become less attentive to Him. We're not as aware of our need for the One who secures our lives and holds us steady until the storms begin to rage. Don't let a few calm breezes give you a false sense of security in yourself and your surroundings. Stay anchored in Christ in gentle times too.

2. *Don't give way to the storm* (see v. 15). Peril caused by another person's poor judgment can often cause feelings of immense helplessness. Don't give way to the storm. Give way to the Master of the seas.

3. *Do throw some cargo overboard* (see v. 18). As the storm worsened, the crew began to jettison cargo to keep the ship afloat. Raging storms have ways of identifying some old stuff we're still hanging on to. When we're upset over someone's poor judgment, we have a tendency to drag up memories of other times we've been wronged as well. Storms complicate life enough. Ask God to simplify and clarify a few things in your life by helping you throw some old cargo overboard.

4. *Do throw the tackle overboard* (see v. 19). After jettisoning the cargo, the crew still needed to further lighten the ship. The tackling on a ship included all kinds of gear: ropes, pulleys, spars, masts, and planks. These objects were man-made provisions needed to master the storm. Storms are seldom pleasant, but they can serve an important purpose. They help us to see the man-made solutions we're substituting in place of depending on and getting to know God.

5. *Never give up hope* (see v. 20). Luke uses the word "we" when identifying those who gave up hope. This is a man who wrote one of the Gospels! How could he lose hope? He had witnessed miracles! This text reminds us that anyone can lose hope when a storm rages. The original word for "gave up" in verse 20 is the same one translated "cutting loose" in verse 40. We might say Luke and the others cut loose their hope when the storm continued to rage day after day. The psalmist offers us a lifesaver in our raging storms in Psalm 62:5: "Rest in God alone, my soul, for my hope comes from Him."

> I cannot promise you everything will be OK. But I promise you based on the faithfulness of God that *you* can be OK.

The "hope" in Psalm 62:5 is the word *tiqvah*, which literally means "a cord, as an attachment" (Strong's). The psalmist contrasted the disappointment he often experienced in man with the security he found in his faithful God. His cord or rope was attached to God alone. We're all holding on to a rope of some kind for security, but if anyone but God is on the other end, we're hanging on by a thread! Hang on to Christ for dear life when the waves break harshly against you. He will be your survival no matter what the storm may destroy. Only He can keep you from becoming bitter. Only He can rebuild what gale-force winds tear apart.

6. *Listen for God to speak* (see v. 24). Incline your ear to the Master of the seas when the storms rage. He will not be silent. Just when the passengers and crew had lost hope, Paul stood to testify. He told them, "This night an angel of the God I belong to and serve stood by me, saying, 'Don't be afraid, Paul. You must stand before Caesar. And, look! God has graciously given you all those who are sailing with you'" (vv. 23–24).

God will probably not send an angel from heaven to speak audibly to you, but He may send a fellow believer, a neighbor, a pastor, or friend. You can also hear Him speak through His Word anytime you are willing to open the Bible and receive.

Job also suffered for reasons outside his control, in ways we will never experience. He had plenty of places to lay blame. I believe one reason he survived such tragedy was because God proved not to be silent as Job had feared. The place in which He spoke to Job is very applicable to us today. Job 40:6 tells us, "The Lord answered Job from the whirlwind." God will speak to you too—straight to your heart. Sometimes others can make decisions that are devastating to our lives. I cannot promise you everything will be OK. It may be; it may not be. But I promise you based on the faithfulness of God that *you* can be OK. Just don't pull up that anchor. And never let go of the rope.

Think of someone you know who's enduring their own blinding storm right now. How could you encourage them with these insights from Paul's life? What are some of our most helpful roles in the lives of those who are in the deepest throes of crisis?

Praying God's Word Today

Lord, there are times when terrors do seem to overtake me like a flood, when the storm winds seem ready to sweep me away at night (Job 27:20). But I know that You have made darkness Your hiding place, dark storm clouds Your canopy around Yourself. You reach down from on high and take hold of me; You pull me out of deep waters (Ps. 18:11, 16). You, Lord, are my Savior in the storm.

Day 66

Under the Umbrella

Before You Begin

Read Acts 27:27–44

Stop and Consider

The soldiers' plan was to kill the prisoners so that no one could swim off and escape. But the centurion kept them from [it] because he wanted to save Paul. (vv. 42–43)

What are some of the blessings you've experienced because of the wisdom and faithfulness of others? ______________________________

____

____

How would it affect your own daily battle with sin and selfishness if you knew that your obedience was as important to those around you as it is to yourself?

____

____

____

Let's allow God to open our eyes to the importance of faithfulness and obedience through a study in contrasts, by seeing that the umbrella of protection or destruction in one man's hand can often cover many heads. The kind of cover these figurative umbrellas provide is not only determined by belief in God versus unbelief, but also by faithfulness versus unfaithfulness.

In Acts 27 God gave Paul an umbrella of protection because of Paul's obedience in ministry. Whether or not the others on board his sinking ship realized it, many were gathered under the umbrella and found safety. But let's take a look at another kind of umbrella in the storm, on display in the familiar account of the prophet Jonah. You'll recall that God called the prophet to go preach deliverance to Nineveh, Israel's bitter enemy. But rather than preach to the people of Nineveh, Jonah ran the other way, booked passage to Tarshish, and wound up in a fishy situation. Consider these similarities between Jonah and Paul:

- Both were Hebrews, had Jewish backgrounds, and believed in the one true God.
- Both were preachers.
- Both were called to preach unpopular messages in pagan cities.
- Both boarded a ship.
- Both experienced a terrible, life-threatening storm.
- Both greatly impacted the rest of the crew.
- Both knew the key to the crew's survival.

Paul and Jonah had many similarities, didn't they? But let's consider a few contrasts between Paul and Jonah. They differed in at least the following ways:

- Paul was compelled to go to Rome; Jonah was repelled by his calling to Nineveh.
- Paul faced many obstacles on his way to Rome, including imprisonment, injustices, inclement weather, and other difficulties; Jonah's only obstacle was himself!

- Paul had to sit and wait for the Lord; Jonah stood and ran from the Lord!
- Paul felt responsibility for the crew, although the calamity was not his fault; Jonah slept while the others worked to survive the calamity he had brought on them.

If you are a child of God, you hold an umbrella in the storm. May the rest of the crew find it an umbrella of blessing.

Paul and Jonah are great characters to compare and contrast because we can relate to both of them! Sometimes we respond with obedience like Paul. Other times we run from God with a sprinter's stride like Jonah, who revealed an amusing cowardice when in Jonah 1:12, the fugitive preacher told the ship's crewmen, "Pick me up and throw me into the sea so it may quiet down for you, for I know that I'm to blame for this violent storm that is against you." Notice he never offered to jump in!

Let's ask a fair question based on their examples: Does prompt obedience really make much difference? When all was said and done, didn't Paul suffer through a terrible storm although he had been entirely obedient? Didn't Jonah get another chance to obey, and an entire city was spared? So . . . what difference does prompt obedience or faithfulness make anyway?

God loves us whether or not we are obedient, but the quality of our Christian lives is dramatically affected by our response. Allow me to point out a big difference between the obedient Christian and the disobedient one, between obedient times and disobedient times. Jesus said, "If you keep My commands you will remain in My love, just as I have kept My Father's commands and remain in His love. I have spoken these things to you so that My joy may be in you and your joy may be complete" (John 15:10–11).

Although Jonah was ultimately obedient and surprisingly successful, you will search in vain for a single hint of joy in his life. Although Paul seemed to suffer at every turn, he had more to say about joy than any other mouthpiece in the Word of God.

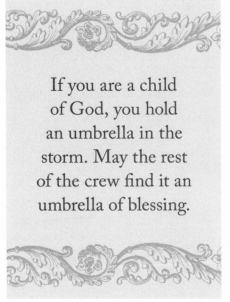

An attitude of obedience makes a difference both to the servant himself and to those close by. Servants of God can dramatically affect the lives of others positively or negatively. Under Jonah's umbrella in the storm, many experienced calamity. Under Paul's umbrella, however, many found safety.

Is the sky rumbling? Are clouds darkening? Is a storm rising in the horizon? If you are a child of God, you will hold an umbrella in the storm. You will not be under the umbrella alone. Neither will I. Our children will be under there with us. Our coworkers may be too. The flocks God has entrusted to us will be there. Even the lost are often drawn to people of faith when hurricane winds begin to blow. Child of God, you and I are centered on the bow of the ship when storms come and the waves crash. May the rest of the crew find an umbrella of blessing in our midst.

What weaknesses of Jonah can you most easily relate to? What strengths of Paul do you most wish to obtain? How has this comparison between the two spoken to your heart?

PRAYING GOD'S WORD TODAY

Lord, You show us in Your Word the example of Abraham, who prayed to You over Sodom, saying, "What if there are 50 righteous people in the city? Will You really sweep it away instead of sparing the place for the sake of the 50 righteous people who are in it? You could not possibly do such a thing: to kill the righteous with the wicked, treating the righteous and the wicked alike. You could not possibly do that! Won't the Judge of all the earth do what is just?" (Gen. 18:24–25). Father, like Your people of old, we humble ourselves, pray and seek Your face, and turn from our evil ways, knowing that You will hear from heaven, forgive our sin, and heal our land (2 Chron. 7:14).

Day 67

Shadows and Snakes

BEFORE YOU BEGIN

Read Acts 28:1–6

STOP AND CONSIDER

They expected that he would swell up or suddenly drop dead. But after they waited a long time and saw nothing unusual happen to him, they changed their minds. (v. 6)

Don't think for one minute that people aren't curious about God, knowing deep inside that He exists and holds some sway. How have you seen evidence of this in them?

What might be some of the reasons why God has chosen to reveal Himself in this way, not knocking people over the head but leaving traces and clues?

One of the vipers indigenous to the region where Paul and his shipmates crashed is a small but poisonous snake. Interestingly, it looks similar to a dead branch when immobile, so in all likelihood Paul picked up the snake as he was gathering brushwood. (Doesn't that just give you the creeps?) When he put the branches in the fire, the viper took the first way out: Paul's hand. Can you imagine what Paul was thinking as the snake dangled from his hand? "Five times I received from the Jews 40 lashes minus one. Three times I was beaten with rods. Once I was stoned. Three times I was shipwrecked" (2 Cor. 11:24–25), *and now this!*

God used the creature, however, to reveal the beliefs of the islanders. Their response to Paul's snakebite was, "This man is probably a murderer, and though he has escaped the sea, Justice does not allow him to live!" (Acts 28:4). Even though their assumption was incorrect, they revealed a limited knowledge of the one true God. Depending on the Bible translation you have, you may have noticed the word "Justice" was capitalized as a proper noun. The original Greek word *dikastes* actually means "a judge, one who executes justice, one who maintains law and equity." Although the island of Malta had presumably never been evangelized, its inhabitants revealed an awareness of a divine judge who maintains justice in the world.

Out of love for the world, God makes Himself known even in the most remote places on earth. Some call this self-disclosure "natural revelation." God desires for people to seek the unknown through the known, discovering a greater knowledge leading to salvation. Paul penned the clear words verifying God's universal declaration of His existence: "From the creation of the world His invisible attributes, that is, His eternal power and divine nature, have been clearly seen, being understood through what He has made. As a result, people are without excuse" (Rom. 1:20).

God is so merciful, isn't He? He doesn't just want people to be without excuse. He doesn't want people to be without a Savior. Justice was the natural light through which the people of Malta first perceived the one true God.

Praying God's Word Today

Lord, You teach us many lessons through the birds of the sky and the fish of the sea. Even the animals make plain that Your hand is active on earth (Job 12:7–9). The heavens, too, declare Your glory, and the sky proclaims the work of Your hands. Day after day they pour out speech; night after night they communicate knowledge. There is no speech; there are no words; their voice is not heard. Their message has gone out to all the earth, and their words to the ends of the inhabited world (Ps. 19:1–4). You have not left us—any of us—beyond reach of Your love and grace. Thank You for choosing to involve Yourself in our needy and fallen lives.

Day 68

Only God

Before You Begin

Read Acts 28:7–10

Stop and Consider

The rest of those on the island who had diseases also came and were cured. So they heaped many honors on us. (v. 9–10)

We've all seen enough concert footage and sporting events to know what adulation looks like. But how should a servant of God handle it when he or she is given recognition?

What has to change inside your heart before you can truly brag on God, before you can take your own contribution out of the mix and genuinely give Him all the glory?

When God performed His awesome, miraculous work on the island of Malta, healing all the sick, I believe His main purpose was to meet their spiritual needs. Three details suggest God worked in the physical realm for spiritual reasons.

First, *Paul prayed* before he healed the chief official's father, not wanting the people of Malta to think he was a god. Prayer helped redirect their attention to the source of all healing—Jesus Christ, the Great Physician.

The second detail that suggests God used physical needs to shed light on spiritual realities was His *means of healing*. He used Paul to heal, yet Luke was a physician. Why? I believe God wanted the people of Malta to recognize God (instead of some well-educated professional) as the source of their healing. No doubt God used Luke many times to tend the sick, but when He wanted to leave no room for doubt, He used someone with no knowledge of medicine.

The last detail that suggests God was up to something spiritual was *wholesale healing*. Sadly, an evangelist may not pack the house with good preaching and Spirit-filled worship, but he can draw large crowds with rumors of healing. Yes, God cares about the sick. He cares deeply. And He often heals physical illnesses, but seldom in Scripture did He use a servant to bring physical healing to an entire land. God used the physical needs of those in Malta to draw attention to the only One who could meet their spiritual needs. He trusted Paul not to take credit for a work only God can do.

We, too, must be careful to give God the glory when He uses us to accomplish things only He can do. Every time you exercise a spiritual gift, God is accomplishing His work through you. If you are a servant of God and you have known Him long, He has used you to do something only He can do.

Think of a work He has accomplished through you. If you're uncomfortable with this request, you may still be taking too much credit. I'm asking you to boast in God, not in yourself. Pray about your availability for any work He might use you to accomplish. Then commit to give Him the glory.

PRAYING GOD'S WORD TODAY

Not to us, Lord, not to us, but to Your name give glory because of Your faithful love, because of Your truth. Why should the nations say, "Where is their God?" (Ps. 115:1–2). May they say instead that they see You in us, that they know Your love by knowing Your children. Please, Lord, make known to those around us the glorious wealth of the gospel, which is Christ in us, the hope of glory (Col. 1:27).

Day 69

Friends in Every Port

BEFORE YOU BEGIN

Read Acts 28:11–14

STOP AND CONSIDER

There we found believers and were invited to stay with them for seven days.
And so we came to Rome. (v. 14)

How important was brotherhood in Christ to the apostle Paul? Was there something unique about his calling or his nature that required this kind of companionship?

How important is brotherhood (or sisterhood) in your own life? If it's not very important, why would you say that's the case? If it is, what are its greatest blessings to you?

In the early spring of AD 61, God fulfilled His promise to Paul. The apostle arrived in Rome. Our text in Acts is very brief and may leave some of us yearning for details. Although Luke wrote about the shipwreck in detail, he did not include Paul's reaction when he reached Rome. Surely he was overwhelmed by the imposing sight, yet more so by his faithful God.

Paul had never seen anything like Rome. At the time of his arrival, Rome was inhabited by one million citizens and approximately the same number of slaves. By even today's standards, the city was gigantic. Rome shared a number of characteristics with many current overcrowded inner cities. Although magnificent buildings and luxurious villas begged to steal the onlooker's attention, he would have to tear his focus from the seas of tenements on the verge of collapse. These four- to five-story *insulae*, with no running water or sanitary restrictions, housed most of the city's population.

As Paul approached the gargantuan city, I believe God knew he would be overwhelmed by a great sea of strangers and the certainty of enemies. Not coincidentally, God met him at each stepping stone to Rome with brothers. Keep in mind that brotherhood in Christ is not a term related to masculinity. It refers to the unique fellowship shared by brothers and sisters in Christ.

Scripture refers to a natural sibling of Paul's only once, yet I counted ninety-nine times in his epistles when the apostle referred to other Christians as brothers. The Greek word for "brothers" is *adelphos*. In reference to fellow believers in Christ, the term "came to designate a fellowship of love equivalent to or bringing with it a community of life." As Paul approached Rome, God knew he needed "a fellowship of love" or "a community of life."

Paul's need was not unique. People are desperate for a sense of community today. We all want to feel like we belong somewhere. God recognizes our need for community and desires to meet the need through His church—the body of believers God organized to offer a community of life.

Praying God's Word Today

Lord Jesus, we know that we have passed from death to life because we love our brothers. For Your Word says that the one who does not love remains in death. This is how we have come to know love: You laid down Your life for us. We should also lay down our lives for our brothers (1 John 3:14, 16). Thank You, Lord, for surrounding us with Your love by surrounding us with Your people—our brothers, our sisters in Christ.

Day 70

Family Obligations

Before You Begin

Read Acts 28:15–16

Stop and Consider

The believers from there had heard the news about us and had come to meet us. . . . When Paul saw them, he thanked God and took courage. (v. 15)

As you think of the community of faith where you worship and the Christian friends you most enjoy being with, what would you say gives you your sense of togetherness?

Where togetherness is lacking, to what would you attribute it? How much of the fault is yours to bear? What do your brothers and sisters really need from you?

Many people believe in Christ as Savior yet never sense a brotherhood or sisterhood with other Christians. In Paul's life, however, I see three strands that formed the cord of brotherhood he felt with other believers.

1. *Paul believed in the power of prayer and in our spiritual poverty without it.* Over and over in his letters, Paul assured churches of his prayers. He didn't just ask God to bless them. Paul jealously sought God's best for them. He asked big things of God because he knew God had big things to give. Paul had experienced the riches of an intimate relationship with Christ. He wanted other believers to experience those same riches.

2. *Paul believed that part of his calling was to share his gifts and faith with other Christians.* He truly believed that Christians have an obligation to one another as well as to the lost. In 1 Corinthians 12:12 he said, "The body is one and has many parts, and all the parts of that body, though many, are one body." Without apology, Paul instructed believers, as "parts" of the "body" of Christ, to recognize their obligation to one another—and their need for one another. Generally speaking, my spiritual gifts were given for your edification; your spiritual gifts were given for mine.

3. *Paul desired to see all people come to Christ.* He preached to anyone who would listen, and he considered any convert a brother or sister. All were equally in need of salvation, and all were equally loved by God. At first consideration we may fully believe we share his attitude, but sometimes we struggle with the equality of all believers. We may desire to see all people saved regardless of their race and position, but we don't necessarily want them to attend church with us.

Paul was greatly encouraged by the brothers who met him in Rome. Their faces were unfamiliar, but they each had been washed in the blood of Jesus Christ. They were family. God used prayer, a sense of mutual obligation, and a sense of equality to bind their hearts. Paul's example teaches us that a sense of community is not derived from the actions and attitudes of others toward us, but from our actions and attitudes toward them. As we imitate his approach to other believers, we will form cords of love not quickly broken.

Praying God's Word Today

Lord, I love how Your Word describes our obligations toward our family in Christ, not in long, persuasive speeches but in simple, direct statements: "Just as I have loved you, you must also love one another" (John 13:34). "Show family affection to one another with brotherly love" (Rom. 12:10). "Love one another earnestly from a pure heart" (1 Pet. 1:22). Therefore, as we have opportunity, help us work for the good of all, especially for those who belong to the household of faith (Gal. 6:10).

Day 71

Retired Faculties

Before You Begin

Read Acts 28:17–29

Stop and Consider

"Therefore, let it be known to you that this saving work of God has been sent to the Gentiles; they will listen!" (v. 28)

How has God continued to supply and equip your spiritual life, even years after your initial salvation experience? ____________________

____

____

Many things continue to remain mysteries to us, but what are one or two bits of spiritual understanding God has given you lately? ____________________

____

____

____

How terribly we cheat ourselves when we have as much as we want from God. Although many of us have received the gift of salvation, in other ways we are not unlike some of the Jews that Paul encountered. We mimic the words of Felix, holding up our hand to God and saying, "That's enough. That's all I'm comfortable with" (see Acts 24:25).

Whatever the reason for our resistance, we may suffer from our own rendition of Paul's diagnosis of many Jews. Based on my own experience, I recognize the danger. At times I've resisted what God wanted to do in me or through me. I seemed to hear Him less, see His activity less, and, tragically, love Him less. Thankfully, when I finally relented and became receptive, my spiritual abilities to hear, see, and love were restored to me.

Let's examine the expressions Paul used and consider the abilities at risk when God desires to give and we continue to resist.

1. *"You will listen and listen, yet never understand"* (Acts 28:26). By the word "listen," Paul referred to the basic physical ability. By the phrase "never understand," he referred to a crippling inability. The Greek word for "understanding" is *suniemi*, meaning "the assembling of individual facts into an organized whole, as collecting the pieces of a puzzle and putting them together." *Suniemi* is exercised when "the mind grasps concepts and sees the proper relationship between them." Do you see the tragedy at stake?

When we continue to resist what God has for us, we may cripple our ability to understand how the pieces of our puzzle fit together. We will constantly single out our experiences rather than understand them as parts of a whole. The things we go through may never make any sense to us. Preachers and teachers may tell us God is at work in our lives, but although we physically hear, we have little ability to understand.

Although we will not understand everything until we see Christ face-to-face, God often blesses us by letting many things make sense during our lifetimes. Most things I've encountered eventually made sense as I developed a more cooperative spirit and a greater understanding of God's purposes. Many of those experiences still hurt, but I find comfort in seeing their eventual usefulness as parts of the whole.

You might think of the process this way: God is faithfully putting a puzzle together in each life so that the final picture will resemble Christ (see Rom. 8:28–29). If we continue to resist this further work, we will be less likely to see the pieces fit.

By heeding Paul's warning, we can have ears willing to hear, eyes willing to see, and hearts willing to be exercised.

2. *"You will look and look, yet never perceive"* (Acts 28:26). Again Paul referred to a basic physical ability as he used the word "look" to mean human vision. "Perceive" is translated from the Greek word *eido*, which merges the ability to see with the ability to know. *Eido* is "not the mere act of seeing, but the actual perception of some object." If we continue to resist the further blessings and works of God in our lives, we may lose some ability to see past the obvious and the physical. Those who allow God to unleash His Holy Spirit in their lives are those who often perceive spiritual and eternal works in the physical and temporal realm. People who never see with spiritual eyes can't comprehend how others claim to see God at work.

I'll never forget the time Amanda's seat belt in our old station wagon wouldn't fasten. Five years old at the time, she pushed and pushed on it to no avail, so I finally told her to crawl into the front seat. Seconds later, the window where she had been sitting inexplicably imploded and pieces of glass imbedded into the seat she had just left. I exclaimed, "Thank You, dear God!"

Later she asked, "Do you really think that was God?"

I said, "No, baby. I *know* that was God." Every now and then God blesses us with a good dose of *eidos*. We not only see—we know! When Paul tried to point out Christ's fulfillment of Old Testament prophecy, many Jews chose to close their eyes and refuse to see. God wants to give us supernatural sight. Let's not resist Him. Our lives are so much richer when we not only see but we also perceive!

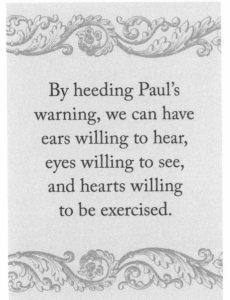

3. "*This people's heart has grown callous*" (Acts 28:27). I was surprised when I discovered the meaning of the word "calloused." You may be too! The original word is *pachuno*, meaning "to make fat . . . calloused as if from fat." According to this verse, people who continue to resist God can develop fat around their hearts. In the physical realm, one reason fat develops around the heart is a lack of exercise. In spiritual matters many of the Jews had ceased exercising their hearts. Religion for them involved more of a state of mind and intellect than the heart.

At one time or another, we've all been hurt in love relationships. But if we cease to exercise our hearts by loving God and loving others, getting involved, and taking risks, our hearts will become diseased and hardened.

Through the prophet Isaiah and the apostle Paul, God revealed three dangers and three opposite blessings. By heeding Paul's warning, we can have ears willing to hear, eyes willing to see, and hearts willing to be exercised.

What are you holding back from God today? In what area of your life are you sensing His loving call to come and trust Him, to open yourself to His will and direction?

PRAYING GOD'S WORD TODAY

How I long, Lord, for my heart not to be hard and insensitive, but rather to delight in Your instruction (Ps. 119:70). Therefore, as You give me the strength and desire, I will rejoice in the way revealed by Your decrees, as much as in all riches. I will meditate on Your precepts and think about Your ways. I will delight in Your statutes; I will not forget Your word (Ps. 119:14–16). I want to be open, Lord, to everything You say, sensitive to every point of correction, becoming more and more like You.

Day 72

Continuous Acts

Before You Begin

Read Acts 28:30–31

Stop and Consider

He welcomed all who visited him, proclaiming the kingdom of God and teaching the things concerning the Lord Jesus Christ with full boldness. (vv. 30–31)

Looking back on the book of Acts, what are some of the top-of-mind remembrances that have made for your greatest lessons in God's ways and His purposes?

We have more to hear from Paul as we venture into his New Testament letters, but what adjectives and observations of his life have struck you as being the most inspiring?

We now conclude our studies in the fascinating book of Acts. I've relished every second of our journey. In a blinding light on the Damascus road, I saw God's mercy. In a midnight song from a dungeon, I heard authentic worship. In every miracle on the island of Malta, I felt hope. The book of Acts has quickened my senses and involved me. I pray that you've also gotten involved. Much more awaits us, but not from the pen of Luke. Our remaining days will take us to the letters Paul wrote during the last six years of his earthly life. But Luke's final account provides a fitting conclusion to the book of Acts.

Recently a friend asked me what impressed me most from my research about Paul. I didn't hesitate to answer. God used the apostle's unparalleled passion for Christ to woo me into the study, then used his inconceivable perseverance to sustain me.

When I was a child, someone gave my brother an inflatable clown with sand in the base. No matter how we socked that clown, he always came back up for more. The apostle was no clown, but every time he got hit, he bounced back up for more. Of course, the reason for his perseverance was his deep passion for Christ.

In these last moments from the book of Acts, we've gotten a glimpse of the risk we take when we put our hand up to God and say, "No more. I'm comfortable this way." We've also realized how much we have to gain by remaining receptive to God. He has so much to give us. Yet His greatest riches are those things that are conformable, not comfortable.

As we conclude the book of Acts, I pray we've each had our eyes unveiled to the extraordinary works God can do in ordinary lives. As we've sojourned from chapter to chapter in Luke's wonderful book, we've met Stephen, Paul, Barnabas, John Mark, Timothy, Silas, Aquila, Priscilla, Philip the evangelist, his four daughters, and many more. They all shared one thing in common: they were simple flesh and blood infiltrated by the awesome power of the Holy Spirit—all because they didn't resist.

We may never leave our native land or travel by sea, as Paul did. But if we love and serve God, our lives will be a great adventure. He'll never take you anywhere He has not already prepared for your arrival. Keep trusting Him. There are more Acts to be performed.

PRAYING GOD'S WORD TODAY

I'm reminded, Lord Jesus, that John said in speaking of Your ministry here, "There are also many other things that Jesus did, which, if they were written one by one, I suppose not even the world itself could contain the books that would be written" (John 21:25). I also believe that whole books could be written about the activity You are performing here this very day. So let all who seek You rejoice and be glad in You; let those who love Your salvation continually say, "God is great!" (Ps. 70:4). Thank You for continuing to use us in Your awesome, mysterious plan for man's redemption.

Day 73

No Kidnapping

BEFORE YOU BEGIN

Read Colossians 2:1–5

STOP AND CONSIDER

I am saying this so that no one will deceive you with persuasive arguments. For I may be absent in body, but I am with you in spirit. (vv. 4–5)

Can you think of a time when Satan tempted you to misappropriate a biblical concept, giving it priority over Christ? How did you realize your error?

How do you observe Satan kidnapping people's minds today—even those of believers—twisting truth in order to lure hearts away from undiluted discipleship?

During Paul's first imprisonment in Rome, he was under what we would call house arrest. Acts 28:30, remember, tells us that "he stayed two whole years in his own rented house. And he welcomed all who visited him." The openness of Paul's first imprisonment in Rome enabled him to receive ample information about the churches. One of the letters he wrote during this two-year period became the book of Colossians. Though as far as we know, Paul never visited the Asian city of Colosse, he obviously received word about the false teaching there and wrote his epistle as both a warning and an encouragement. You would benefit most by reading all four chapters of Colossians. If you choose one chapter, the primary purpose for Paul's epistle appears in Colossians 2.

Paul made one primary purpose for the letter clear in verse 4: "so that no one will deceive you." Have you, or someone you know, ever been taken captive through some deceptive philosophy? Our world is replete with those who seek to control others through false and deceptive beliefs.

Try to capture Paul's frame of mind as he wrote the Christians in Colosse. He described himself as being in a great "struggle" (v. 1). The Greek word is *agon*, from which we derive the English word "agony." *Agon* means "strife, contention, contest for victory or mastery such as was used in the Greek games of running, boxing, wrestling, and so forth." By using the word *agon*, Paul implied that he was figuratively boxing or wrestling with Satan for the minds and hearts of the Colossians and Laodiceans. No sooner had the people of Colosse and Laodicea received the Word of God than Satan began infiltrating them with deceptive doctrines. Satan used at least four "isms." Let's briefly consider each one.

1. *Gnosticism.* The word *gnosis* means "knowledge." Followers of the gnostic belief system believed that knowledge, rather than faith, led to salvation. We risk something of the same problem if we focus on knowledge instead of Christ. We need to study the Bible to know and glorify Jesus rather than to impress others with our knowledge. I once heard a friend utter a prayer I have not forgotten. She said, "Lord, we know You desire followers who have hearts like a cathedral rather than minds like a concordance."

Since the gnostics prioritized intellect and reason, they tried to force God into humanly understandable form. They could not accept both the deity and the humanity of Christ, so they tried to reduce Him to the status of an angel. Paul responded to gnosticism clearly in verse 9: "For in Him [in Christ] the entire fullness of God's nature dwells bodily."

> Satan is still up to the same old tricks. He seeks always to infiltrate the church with his false teaching.

2. *Legalism.* Paul addressed the fruitlessness of keeping endless laws that condemn rather than liberate the believer to pursue godliness. We humans constantly attempt to replace a love relationship with legalistic requirements such as:

- seeking to be more spiritual than others by keeping man-made, extrabiblical rules
- believing that God requires harsh treatment of the body
- elevating one Christian above another
- refusing to accept those who have committed certain sins
- attempting to restrain sin by lists of dos and don'ts

No matter how ingeniously humans pursue legalism, it will never work. Only a love relationship with Christ can change the human heart and bring about genuine piety.

3. *Mysticism.* This is the belief that we can obtain direct knowledge of God from our internal thoughts, feelings, or experiences. It conflicts with biblical faith because Jesus Christ is the source of our knowledge about God. In verses 18 and 19, Paul addressed a mystical belief that has recently infiltrated our own society—the worship of angels. Angels certainly have important positions in God's creation, but Paul helps us find the balance. Angels were created to praise God and act as messengers and ministering servants. We worship angels when we disconnect them from their original purpose, focusing on them alone outside of their place in God's created order.

4. *Asceticism.* In verses 20 through 23, Paul addressed the practice of denying the body and treating it harshly in an attempt to achieve holiness. Followers of asceticism do not stop at the wise denial of dangerous, perverse, or unhealthy practices. Ascetics deny the body unnecessarily. In Paul's day, as in ours, some people branded, burned, starved, or cut themselves in an attempt to force the body into submission. Most of us have discovered that unnecessary denial arouses more desires.

We still battle many of the same destructive philosophies faced by the early believers. Though the list of "isms" may change, Satan is still up to the same old tricks. He seeks always to infiltrate the church with his false teaching.

How do we defend ourselves against these subtle attacks of the enemy? How should we confront those who are peddling them, and how can we best seek to be a corrective influence on those who are falling under their spell? ______________________________

Praying God's Word Today

Lord God, when You asked the woman in the Garden, "What is this you have done?" her response was, "It was the serpent. He deceived me, and I ate" (Gen. 3:13). Just as Eve was deceived by the serpent's cunning, the minds of even those with a complete and pure devotion to Christ can be corrupted and led astray (2 Cor. 11:3). Please help me to always be aware of what my enemy is up to. Help me not to be deceived by the serpent's cunning.

Day 74

Keep Your Guard Up

BEFORE YOU BEGIN

Read Colossians 2:6–15

STOP AND CONSIDER

As you have received Christ Jesus the Lord, walk in Him, rooted and
built up in Him and established in the faith, just as you were taught. (vv. 6–7)

Flesh out the verse above, applying it to your own life. What specific actions could you take to improve your grounding, your development, your establishment in the faith?

You may feel anywhere from "not at all" to "somewhat" to "totally" confident in helping others grow in Christ. Still, what's a way that you could be helpful in another's maturity?

Once we accept Christ as Savior, we become joint heirs with Christ (see Rom. 8:17), and God becomes our Father (see John 20:17). Satan may try to kidnap us by enticing us away from the truth, but no matter what he does, he cannot make us his. Let's discover how to protect ourselves from being lured away by "empty deceit" (Col. 2:8).

1. *Remember how you received Christ.* None of us entered God's family through our own effort. We received Christ as a gift of grace. Now Paul tells us that the way we got in is the way we go on. We must not believe any teaching or philosophy that replaces God's grace with our performance.

2. *Continue to live in Christ.* The best way for a child of God to avoid being kidnapped is to stay close to home. Children in natural families cannot live their entire lives in their yards, but children in the spiritual family of God can! Continuing to live in Christ means remaining close to Him and retaining a focus on Him. Any other focus can lead to deceptive doctrine, even if the focus is a biblical concept. Remember, any doctrine that loses connection with the Head has been twisted into deception. Many of us have probably let something temporarily become a greater focus than Christ Himself. I've seen people make a specific belief or detail of doctrine such a focus. We are less likely to be kidnapped when we stay close to home by staying focused on the Head, Jesus Christ.

3. *Grow deep roots in Christ.* The more we feel like family, the less likely we'll be enticed. An important part of feeling like family is knowing your family history and the belief systems handed down through the generations. Spiritually, we have difficulty growing up until we've grown down. We form deep roots by knowing the basics of our faith. We can receive Christ and be enthusiastic and still fall into confusion the first time someone confronts us with strange doctrine. Our roots are our basics.

4. *Grow up in Christ.* In verse 7, the apostle exhorted believers to be "rooted and built up in Him." After we've grown roots, we're ready to grow up. Hebrews 6:1 strongly exhorts believers to a progression in Christ: "Therefore, leaving the elementary message about the Messiah, let us go on to maturity." All of these keep us from being easy targets.

Praying God's Word Today

Lord Jesus, I desire to become mature, growing to a stature measured only by Your faithfulness. Then I will no longer be like a little child, tossed by the waves and blown around by every wind of teaching, by human cunning with cleverness in the techniques of deceit. Help me, Lord, to speak the truth in love, growing in every way into You, the head of the church (Eph. 4:13–15)—the source of my very existence.

Day 75

Submitted and Free

Before You Begin

Read Ephesians 5:22–24

Stop and Consider

Wives, submit to your own husbands as to the Lord, for the husband is head of the wife as also Christ is head of the church. (vv. 22–23)

I'm giving you permission here to write down (or talk about) anything this verse and this concept stirs in your mind. Whatcha got? ______

______

______

Fair and balanced, write down anything derived from this biblical admonition that could be reclassified as a blessing. What makes submission a good thing? ______

______

______

______

For the next few days, we will concentrate on the letter to the Ephesians. Most scholars believe Colossians and Ephesians were written early in Paul's two-year imprisonment in Rome because he never hinted of a possible release as he did in Philemon (see v. 22) and Philippians (see 1:19–26).

The letter to the Ephesians differs from his letter to the Colossians. Paul never warned of deceptive philosophy; rather, he wrote about a greater knowledge and experience in Christ. We can easily deduce the reason for the omission of several basics. Remember, the Christians at Colosse had never met Paul, while the people of Ephesus had benefited from his teaching and an unparalleled demonstration of power for several years.

Paul found receptive soil in Ephesus, even in the midst of terrible hardships. His lengthy and effective ministry in Ephesus not only resulted in deep bonds of love and brotherhood (see Acts 20:37–38); it also freed him to proceed to great depths in his letter. Space limits me to choose only one or two subjects from the book of Ephesians, but among the most important are the biblical roles of three distinct figures intimately involved in marriage: wives, husbands, and Christ. Ladies, let's get the painful part over first!

First, look back to verse 21, where Paul speaks of "submitting to one another in the fear of Christ." The attitude of all Christians is to be submissive to one another. No discussion of this topic can stay on track apart from that spirit. Paul's primary directive to women dealt with submission, while his primary directive to men dealt with love. Could it be that he was targeting the areas most likely to be our weaknesses? Before we learn what submission means for Christian wives, let's learn what it does not mean:

1. *Submission does not mean women are under the authority of men in general.* I love the King James Version's rendition of Ephesians 5:22: "Wives, submit yourselves unto your own husbands." Guess what? Wives aren't asked to submit to anyone else's husband—just their own! While I make this point somewhat tongue-in-cheek, many women assume the Bible teaches their general inferiority and subjection to men. Untrue. Paul is talking about marriage as a matter between each husband and wife.

2. *Submission does not mean inequality.* Paul, the same man who taught submission, made a statement in Galatians 3:28 pertinent to our subject: "There is no Jew or Greek, slave or free, male or female; for you are all one in Christ Jesus." Spiros Zodhiates' definition of the Greek word *hupotasso* explains that submission "is not due to her being inferior to her husband, for they are both equal before God."

God granted women a measure of freedom in submission that we can learn to enjoy.

3. *Submission does not mean wives are to treat their husbands like God.* One commentary explains: "'As to the Lord' does not mean that a wife is to submit to her husband in the same way she submits to the Lord, but rather that her submission to her husband is her service rendered 'to the Lord.'"[15] I think most husbands would be relieved to know they are not called on to be God to their wives!

4. *Submission does not mean slavery.* Let's release a few old notions and fears here! Paul uses an entirely different word in Ephesians 6:5 when he instructs slaves to obey their masters. This Greek word for "obey," *hupakouo*, embraces more of the meaning people often mistakenly associate with marital submission. *Hupakouo* means "to obey, to yield to a superior command or force (without necessarily being willing)." The term draws a picture of a soldier saluting his commander, not a wife submitting to her husband!

Now that we've learned a few things submission does not mean, just exactly what *does* it mean? The Greek word for "submit" is *hupotasso. Hupo* means "under" and *tasso* means "to place in order." The compound word *hupotasso* means "to place under or in an orderly fashion." Paul didn't dislike women; he liked order! He advocated order in the church, order in government, order in business, and, yes, order in the home. I'm convinced he even kept his cell in order! Galatians 3:28 and Ephesians 5:22 could spill from the same man's pen because Paul regarded husbands and wives as spiritual equals, though with certain obvious and functional differences.

The concept of a submissive wife really used to go against my grain until I began to learn more about God. Two realizations have changed my entire attitude:

- *God is good and loving.* He would never give approval to meanness or abuse. Any misuse of submission by either the husband or wife is sin.
- *God granted women a measure of freedom in submission that we can learn to enjoy.* It is a relief to know that as a wife and mother, I am not totally responsible for my family. I have a husband I can look to for counsel and direction. I can rely on his manly toughness when I am too soft, and I can rely on his logic when I am too emotional.

Certainly I haven't just delivered the definitive dissertation on submission, but I do believe I'm offering you sound doctrine. I hope it helps.

Think of a way you could affirm your acceptance of this truth in a way that would deepen your relationship with Christ and encourage your husband, all at the same time. How might it change things in your marriage . . . for the better . . . for both of you?

PRAYING GOD'S WORD TODAY

Father, You led Your children, the Israelites, all the way in the desert for forty years, to humble them and to test them in order to know what was in their hearts, whether or not they would keep Your commands (Deut. 8:2). Help me to understand that sometimes You lead me on certain paths to humble me also and to see what is in my heart. Purify my heart, Lord, so that You will take joy in what You find.

Day 76

Love and Marriage

Before You Begin

Read Ephesians 5:25–33

Stop and Consider

Husbands, love your wives, just as also Christ loved the church and gave Himself for her, to make her holy, cleansing her in the washing of water by the word. (vv. 25–26)

Your husband is every bit as commanded to love you as you are commanded to submit to him. But what are some things you could do to help his obedience be more forthcoming?

How does it affect your commitment to marriage by seeing that God is using even yours to demonstrate to the world the mystery of Christ's relationship with His church?

In light of what we considered yesterday, Paul probably had the Ephesian Christians nodding their heads in agreement. Submission of the wife to the husband was codified Hebraic law. Nothing new here. Now Paul raised eyebrows in a hurry. He told husbands to love their wives.

For a society where women were little more than property, passed from father to husband, this command to love their wives was a radical idea. Paul knew few role models existed for the men to follow. He gave them the best role model possible: Jesus Christ.

1. *Husbands should love their wives sacrificially.* Just as a husband must be careful not to abuse his wife's exhortation to submission, a wife must not abuse her husband's exhortation to sacrifice. Some men work several jobs sacrificing time at home in a continual effort to raise the standard of living for their families.

2. *Husbands should love their wives in ways that encourage purity.* Christ encourages purity in His bride, the church, desiring for her to be holy and without stain. God calls upon husbands to treat their wives as pure vessels even in physical intimacy.

3. *Husbands should "love their wives as their own bodies"* (v. 28). I have to snicker when I think about verses 28 and 29. I wonder if Paul might have been thinking, "If you love yourself at all, mister, then love your wife—because life will be far more pleasant under the same roof with a well-loved woman!" I also have to wonder if Paul's reference to a man treating his wife as he does his own body, such as feeding and caring for it, implies that husbands are supposed to cook for their wives. I'm not certain about that interpretation, but I would submit to my husband's cooking any day!

Think of marriage as a three-legged stool—a submissive wife, a loving husband, and Christ. All three must be in place for marriage to work as God intended. A wife submitting to an unloving husband is as lopsided as a loving husband sacrificing for a domineering wife. When Christ is not the head of the marriage, the stool falls indeed. Sadly, many Christian women are trying to keep their stools balanced with only one leg in place—their submission. Pray that your husband would love you out of his devotion to Christ.

Praying God's Word Today

O Lord, I know that if I speak the languages of men and of angels, but do not have love, I am a sounding gong or a clanging cymbal. If I have the gift of prophecy, and understand all mysteries and all knowledge, and if I have all faith, so that I can move mountains, but do not have love, I am nothing. And if I donate all my goods to feed the poor, and if I give my body to be burned, but do not have love, I gain nothing (1 Cor. 13:1–3). Above all, Lord, teach us—teach me—to put on love, the perfect bond of unity (Col. 3:14).

Day 77

Battle Lines

Before You Begin

Read Ephesians 6:10–13

Stop and Consider

Our battle is not against flesh and blood, but against the rulers, against the authorities, against the world powers of this darkness, against the spiritual forces of evil. (v. 12)

What kind of battles are the hottest in your life right now? How do they differ from some of the struggles you've experienced in the past? ______________________

What happens in our hearts when we forget that the enemy we face is very real, very adept, and very intent on taking us under? ______________________

We approach this day as a battalion of soldiers in the middle of a heavenly war. Lives are at risk. Casualties may be high. Our Commander in Chief issues orders. The victory is sure, but the fight will be difficult. Hear the voice of your Commander as He exhorts you to do the following:

1. *Realize your natural limitations.* We cannot enjoy spiritual victory without actively calling on the power of God. We are only strong when we are "strengthened by the Lord and by His vast strength" (v. 10).

2. *Remember the "full armor"* (v. 11). Paul exhorted us to use every weapon available. Picture your Commander in Chief standing behind a table displaying six tools or weapons. He says, "I've tailor-made each of these for you. You may take only some of them if you choose, but they were designed to work together. Your safety and effectiveness are only guaranteed if you use them all." Trust me when I tell you that after at least six thousand years of practice on human targets, your enemy won't waste arrows on well-armed places. He will aim for the spots you and I leave uncovered. I know it from experience.

3. *Recognize your real enemies.* The struggles of warfare you and I experience do not originate in spouses, in-laws, neighbors, coworkers, or any earthly foe. Spiritual forces of evil exist. Not every problem we have is warfare, of course. Sometimes the prescription is repentance from sin. Other times, however, it is fortification against the evil one.

4. *Realize our enemies' limitations.* Satan and his powers and principalities cannot do anything they want with us. They have certain limitations. We can "resist" them, as Paul says in verse 13. Demons can oppress, but they cannot possess, for "when you heard the word of truth, the gospel of your salvation—in Him when you believed—[you] were sealed with the promised Holy Spirit" (Eph. 1:13). He has "sealed you for the day of redemption" (Eph. 4:30). Therefore, Satan cannot read your mind (though he can often guess what you're thinking from past behavior). Walk in the freedom of knowing that when you received Christ, God dropped His Holy Spirit into you, slammed on the lid, and tightened the cap. Nothing can get in. Not even the enemy of your soul.

Praying God's Word Today

I rejoice in You, Lord; I delight in Your deliverance. My very bones say, "Lord, who is like You, rescuing the poor from one too strong for him, the poor or the needy from one who robs him?" (Ps. 35:9–10). Yes, You have rescued me from my powerful enemy and from those who hated me, for they were too strong for me. They confronted me in the day of my distress, but You, Lord, were my support (Ps. 18:17–18). You are my shelter, my portion in the land of the living (Ps. 142:5).

Day 78

Armor All

Before You Begin

Read Ephesians 6:14–20

Stop and Consider

In every situation take the shield of faith, and with it you will be able to extinguish the flaming arrows of the evil one. (v. 16)

What do we mean when we say that we wish life wasn't such a battle? Why do you think God has chosen to leave us in a fighting posture?

What have you learned in battle that you'd never have learned any other way? How has it prepared you for what you're facing now, or for what you may yet face in the future?

When we stopped reading at Ephesians 4:13 yesterday, we were left with the encouragement to "take your stand." Satan definitely wants to force us off our property and make us feel like we're getting nowhere. But God has given us the privilege of standing in the victorious space He desires for us. And He has given us His mighty armor with which to join together with one another in spiritual combat against the enemy. You've most likely studied this list of weaponry before, but as Peter believed, it is valuable to "remind you about these things, even though you know them and are established in the truth you have" (2 Pet. 1:12). May we continue to learn while we live, and fight while we have strength.

The belt of truth represents not living a lie in any part of our lives, living free of secret areas of hypocrisy. Satan loves to blackmail believers who have a secret they want to keep hidden.

The breastplate of righteousness is the protection we receive when we choose the right thing even when we feel like choosing the wrong thing. Not only will we find protection from disaster, God will honor our obedience by changing our hearts if we'll let Him. We will find great protection in learning to pray Psalm 141:4: "Do not let my heart turn to any evil thing."

Feet readied with the gospel of peace. The word for "readiness" is *hetoimasia*, meaning "firm footing." Roman soldiers' boots had cleats on the soles to give them firm footing. Our feet give our bodies balance. We can remain balanced because, although we are at war with Satan, we are at peace with God. Sink your feet into "the gospel of peace"!

The shield of faith is our protection when Satan tempts us to disbelieve God. A big difference separates doubting what God may do and doubting God. Even when you have no idea what God is doing, your protection is in never doubting God is God. We're not called to have faith in our faith. We are called to have faith in God and never doubt Him.

The helmet of salvation protects our minds. The best way to protect our mind is to fill it with the Word of God and things pertaining to godliness. We need to deliberately avoid destructive influences.

The sword of the Spirit. You've probably noticed the defensive nature of all five previous weapons. The sword of the Spirit is our only offensive weapon against the evil one. Christ demonstrated how to be an expert swordsman. In His wilderness temptation Jesus attacked Satan with the Word of God until the enemy gave up. Know and use the Word of God persistently!

> You and I must actively guard the gains we've made in Christ. Paul exhorts us to stand our ground!

Active, anytime prayer. Retain an active prayer life. "Pray at all times in the Spirit" (v. 18). Prayerless lives are powerless lives. Active prayer lives equip us with the power and motivation to put on the full armor of God. Because Paul mentioned praying for others next, I believe this first exhortation was primarily about praying for ourselves.

Prayer for other believers. Remember one another in warfare prayer "with all perseverance and intercession for all the saints," (v. 18). Power results from collective prayer. God delights in our petitions for each other. Soldiers depend on one another to watch their backs! Not long ago I realized I was having an internal problem with anger. I was caught off guard because ordinarily I do not struggle with anger. I prayed many times; finally I shared my struggles with a friend. She began to join me in prayer, and the anger ceased immediately. I cannot explain why. I only know that Satan's secret was out, prayer doubled, and God acted.

Prayer for spiritual leaders. Notice Paul ended by asking for prayer—"Pray also for me" (v. 19). Again, I believe he was talking about warfare prayer because he asked specifically for intercession regarding fearlessness. According to 2 Timothy 1:7, God does not give us a spirit of fear. Satan is the one who fuels fear in an attempt to keep people from serving God effectively. If the great apostle needed prayer to fulfill his calling fearlessly, we all need prayer! Our missionaries, pastors, leaders, and teachers need our prayers. The enemy wants to destroy ministries. Our prayers help build a hedge of protection around them.

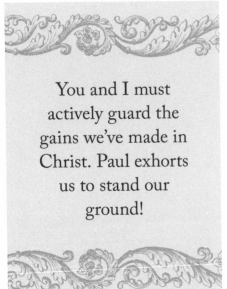

The following list includes each of the exhortations about warfare we've considered today. As you read the list, mentally evaluate yourself on each of the actions.

- I reject personal hypocrisy (the belt of truth).
- I resist snares of unrighteousness (the breastplate of righteousness).
- I remain balanced (feet readied with the gospel of peace).
- I refuse unbelief (the shield of faith).
- I reinforce my mind (the helmet of salvation).
- I raise my sword (the sword of the Spirit).
- I retain an active prayer life.
- I remember others in warfare prayer.
- I specifically remember spiritual leaders in warfare prayer.

What a set of goals! Warfare is a reality for the Christian life. We can do nothing to change that. We can, however, decide whether to be victims or victors.

Take one or two of the challenges from the list above, and think about how you could specifically put them into daily practice, starting right now. ______________________

____

____

____

____

PRAYING GOD'S WORD TODAY

My faithful God, I know that as a lion growls over its prey when a band of shepherds is called out against it, and is not terrified by their shouting or subdued by their noise, so You, the Lord of Hosts will come down to fight against Your enemies. Like hovering birds, so You will protect Your people. By protecting them, You will rescue them; by sparing them, You will deliver them (Isa. 31:4–5). We trust in Your ferocious protection.

Day 79

Growing in Grace

BEFORE YOU BEGIN

Read Philemon 1–10

STOP AND CONSIDER

I, Paul, as an elderly man and now also as a prisoner of Christ Jesus,
appeal to you for my child, whom I fathered while in chains—Onesimus. (vv. 9–10)

As people age, they tend toward one of two extremes—growing hard and unbending, or becoming kinder and more forgiving. What causes us to go one way or the other?

Looking at this common fork in the road of life, which way would you say *you're* heading? How has evidence for either one shown up in your life?

In the last years of the apostle's life, four out of five of his letters were written to individuals rather than to bodies of believers. One of these was addressed to Philemon, a believer from Colosse whom Paul probably met while ministering in a nearby city. Quite possibly Paul had been the one who had personally introduced Philemon to the Savior. They developed a friendship, and Paul saw Philemon become an active worker for the gospel. Philemon must have been a wealthy man to own a home large enough to serve as a meeting place for the church (see v. 2) as well as being a slave owner.

At some time in the intervening years, one of these slaves—Onesimus—had run away, apparently stealing from Philemon in the process. And by the providence of God, he had found himself in Rome, where he met Paul. We have no way of knowing for certain, but perhaps while he was on the run, Onesimus may have stolen again and been incarcerated with Paul. Either way, imagine how strange their meeting must have been once they realized they both knew Philemon. You can be sure their meeting wasn't a coincidence. God had ordained the fugitive slave to have a heart-to-heart collision with the most well-known slave of grace in all Christendom. Paul told him about Christ, and the runaway slave became a brother. Then Paul sent Onesimus back to Philemon with the letter that bears his name.

I am a hopeless romantic. I hate conflict, and I love happy endings. Of all the encounters we've studied, the conflict between Paul and Barnabas was one of the most difficult. I had grown to love the partnership between them so much. My heart ached over their disagreement about John Mark. Twelve years after that event, Paul was placed under house arrest in Rome. Now we see Mark with him once again (see v. 24).

You may be wondering why I am focusing on Paul and Mark when this letter is so obviously about Paul and Onesimus. I think Mark may have been Paul's inspiration for seeking restoration between Philemon and Onesimus. A dozen years earlier Paul had been hard and unyielding. But time heals and, if we're the least bit cooperative, it matures us. Sometimes we live and learn. Perhaps he had since learned a more excellent way.

PRAYING GOD'S WORD TODAY

In You, Christ Jesus, and by Your blood, we who were far away from You have been brought near, for You are our peace. You have united Your people and torn down the dividing wall of hostility that existed between us (Eph. 2:13–14). May we, then, as sons and daughters of Yours, extend to others this wisdom that is from above, a wisdom that is first pure, then peace-loving, gentle, compliant, full of mercy and good fruits, without favoritism and hypocrisy—that the fruit of righteousness will be sown in peace by those of us who make peace (James 3:17–18).

Day 80

For Love's Sake

BEFORE YOU BEGIN

Read Philemon 11–22

STOP AND CONSIDER

Perhaps this is why he was separated from you . . . so that you might get him back permanently, no longer as a slave, but more than a slave—as a dearly loved brother. (vv. 15–16)

Perhaps you're in a situation or facing a decision right now where you're not sure what to do. What would your next move be if you decided to operate purely from love?

____

____

How have you benefitted from another person's decision to treat you with love and mercy, even though you likely deserved much less? ______________________________

____

____

____

Paul could have dealt with this situation between Philemon and Onesimus in one of several different ways, but the wise apostle chose the most excellent way, portraying a beautiful example of Micah 6:8: "He has showed you, O man, what is good. And what does the Lord require of you? To act justly and to love mercy and to walk humbly with your God" (NIV).

More than sacrifices or offerings, God desires these three things from us: to act justly, to love mercy, and to walk humbly with Him. The solution Paul sought in the conflict between Philemon and his fugitive slave, Onesimus, met all three requirements.

1. *Paul acted justly.* One way Paul might have handled this was to consider Onesimus absolved from all responsibility after he repented and accepted Christ. But Onesimus had wronged Philemon in several ways. He had run away from his legal owner and possibly had stolen from him. In Paul's estimation the restoration of two Christian men was priority. The issue could not be resolved fully unless Onesimus returned to Philemon and unless Philemon was repaid for all Onesimus owed.

For justice to prevail, someone had to take responsibility for Onesimus's actions, and someone had to pay his debt. Paul insisted that Onesimus take responsibility for wrongdoing, yet Paul took on the debt (see v. 18). Likewise we must take responsibility for our sins, but thankfully Christ has paid the debt!

2. *Paul loved mercy.* Paul did more than preach to people. He lived the concepts he taught. When he met Onesimus, he saw a man in need of a Savior. Paul didn't just preach to him about the mercy of God, he showed it to him. He took Onesimus's debt not only out of justice but also out of mercy, because a sinner needed grace. Paul wanted Philemon to show mercy as well. According to the original language, Onesimus was a slave bound into permanent servitude to Philemon. His return to Philemon would mean the return to slavery.

Critics of God's Word often protest that the Bible seems to support evils like slavery, but in fact the opposite is true. Jesus and Paul could have come preaching against the specific evils of their day, such as slavery. If they had done so, the message of heart transformation through forgiveness of sin would have been lost. Instead both Christ and Paul concentrated on getting people into a right relationship with God. They knew that evil social institutions would fall before the force of people with the heart of the Father beating in their chests.

The hollowness of works without love becomes evident to all who seek to serve God.

Although Paul had to deal with slavery realistically as a part of his society, he believed in absolute equality. He believed that slaves must be obedient to their masters just like citizens must obey the law, but he was definitely not an advocate of slavery. He told Philemon he was returning Onesimus to him "no longer as a slave, but more than a slave—as a dear loved brother" (v. 16).

God has strong feelings about mercy. In the Old Testament God demanded mercy on slaves. God required His people to remember they also had been slaves and to have mercy on others. As Christ's ambassador, Paul did not violate the Old Testament principle. He had the full cooperation of Onesimus, who was willing to return so restoration would ensue. Paul also asked Philemon to be an ambassador of Christ by abolishing Onesimus's slavery and receiving him as a brother. Paul's proposal was to let mercy reign.

3. Paul walked humbly with God. The closer we draw near to God and the more we behold His majesty, the more we relate to the psalmist who said, "What is man that you are mindful of him?" (Ps. 8:4). Like the psalmist, Paul recognized the pit from which God had pulled him. Both enjoyed an intimate relationship with God, yet neither of them viewed Him as a chum or a running buddy. They each knew grace had bridged the wide gulf fixed between them. To walk with God is to walk humbly. We cannot help but confront His holiness. Paul's proposal for restoration between Philemon and Onesimus required both men to walk humbly with God.

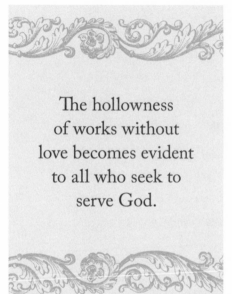

Paul had to humble himself as well by resisting the temptation to be bold and order Philemon to do what he ought to do (vv. 8–9). Instead, he appealed to him on another basis, which brings us to our final point. When God sent His Son to be an atoning sacrifice for our sins, He fulfilled the law with love (see Rom. 5:8). Paul could have demanded certain actions from Philemon, but he appealed to him on the basis of love.

The hollowness of works without love becomes evident to all who seek to serve God. We cannot serve God wholeheartedly without the whole heart. Even though many years earlier Paul and Barnabas had probably made the right decision to divide and multiply, I'm not sure Paul responded to the conflict with John Mark in love. I think a hollowness accompanied Paul everywhere he went until the gulf was bridged with grace. He showed it by personal example to others like Philemon and us.

What are some of the life lessons you've learned from your own mistakes? How has Christ grown and developed you the longer you've been in relationship with Him?

Praying God's Word Today

Lord, I know that from You the whole body—Your people, Your church—fitted and knit together by every supporting ligament, promotes the growth of the body for building up itself in love by the proper working of each individual part. Therefore, may we no longer walk in the futility of our thoughts, darkened in our understanding, excluded from the life of God because of the ignorance that is in us and because of the hardness of our hearts. (Eph. 4:16–18). Rather, by the help of Your Holy Spirit, may our every action be done in love (1 Cor. 16:14). Change us, Lord. Make us more like You.

Day 81

The Secret of His Success

Before You Begin

Read Philippians 4:1–13

Stop and Consider

Do what you have learned and received and heard and seen in me,
and the God of peace will be with you. (v. 9)

What is currently doing the best job of challenging your sense of contentment? Perhaps it's a person. Perhaps it's a work situation. Perhaps it's a health scare. What's it doing to you?

How would the choice—the secret—of contentment affect the way you're handling this? Even if nothing changed, even if it got worse, what would be changing inside of *you?*

How many truly contented people do you know? They are rare gems, aren't they? The enemy loves to see our discontentment because contented Christians live a powerful and effective testimony. Their lives are walking witnesses, proving that Christ can deliver what the gods of this world can't. You can be sure of this: wherever one of these rare gems exist, a jewel thief is lurking close by.

We can identify the following five thieves of contentment based on Philippians 4:

1. *Pettiness.* To everyone who thought the apostle Paul did not believe in women in ministry, allow me to introduce Euodia and Syntyche: "I urge Euodia and I urge Syntyche to agree in the Lord. . . . Help these women who have contended for the gospel at my side" (Phil. 4:2–3). They worked right beside him. They were fellow workers! They had just one little problem: they couldn't get along. Let's admit it: people can be petty!

God intentionally made women sensitive. But I believe the counterfeit of sensitivity is pettiness. We tend to get our feelings hurt easily and take things personally. God gave us a special tenderness and sensitivity to lend a sweetness to our service. Pettiness, however, sours a servant's heart and steals contentment.

2. *Anxiety.* I personally can't think of a more successful jewel thief. Paul counters, "Don't worry about anything, but in everything, through prayer and petition with thanksgiving, let your requests be made known to God" (Phil. 4:6). No anxiety—what a thought! How do we turn off the valve that is pumping anxiety into our souls? Paul proposes an answer: prayer. You might say, "A better solution to fighting anxiety must exist. I've prayed—and still been anxious." I want to suggest gently that you haven't necessarily been practicing the kind of prayer Paul was describing as a prescription for anxiety.

Verse 6 describes an intimate and active prayer life. Notice Paul's words for prayer and supplication. The word "prayer" refers to a very general kind of prayer. The word "petition" or "supplication" is translated from the Greek word *deesis,* describing a very personal kind of prayer. *Deesis* is "the petition for specific individual needs and wants." Paul exhorted believers to come to God with general requests and needs as well as the details that cause us anxiety. And don't give up! Persist until peace comes. Keep praying not only about your critical needs but about everything! An open line of communication with God reminds you He is real and active in your life, and the peace that overflows lends contentment.

> I believe Paul considered reliance on God a secret because everyone has to discover it for themselves.

3. *Destructive thinking*. Proverbs 23:7 describes man with the words, "For as he thinks within himself, so he is." We might say a person feels like he or she thinks. Our human natures tend toward negative and destructive thoughts. If ten people complimented you today and one person criticized, which would you go to bed thinking about tonight? Probably the criticism!

Destructive, negative thinking is a habit that can be broken, but this thief takes diligence to overcome. God knows the tendency of the mind to think and rethink on a certain subject, meditating on things. Paul gave us a wonderful checklist for determining whether our thoughts are worth thinking! "Whatever is true, whatever is honorable, whatever is just, whatever is pure, whatever is lovely, whatever is commendable . . . dwell on these things" (Phil. 4:8).

I struggle with destructive thinking just like you do. God has used Scripture memory and Bible study to set me free. I continue to make His Word a daily priority, but He also blesses the refreshment I gain from the occasional decent movie, a wholesome magazine, a good documentary, or a funny book. Worthy thought patterns are a key to contentment.

4. *Resistance to learn*. Paul said, "I have learned to be content in whatever circumstances I am" (v. 11). No one was born with contentment. Paul learned from experience that God was faithful no matter what circumstance he met. Had he never been in want, He never would have learned! Often we're in no mood to learn when we're in difficult circumstances, but God desires to show us that we can't meet a circumstance He can't handle. We handcuff a sly thief of contentment when we ask God to give us hearts willing to learn.

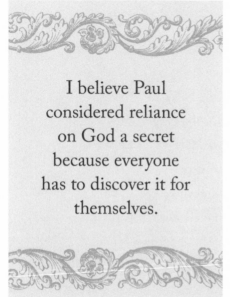

5. *Independence.* Refusing to rely on God robs us of some of God's most priceless riches. Through countless ups and downs, Paul learned he could do everything God called him to do, but only "through Him who strengthens me" (v. 13). Through the multitude of needs Paul encountered, he learned that "God will supply all your needs according to His riches in glory in Christ Jesus" (v. 19). I believe Paul considered reliance on God a secret because everyone has to discover it for themselves. I can tell you God will meet your every need. I can say that you can do all things through Christ; but until you find out for yourself, it's still a secret. I can tell you, but He will show you. Let Him. He is so faithful.

Contentment is a rare gem. Because Paul ceased letting thieves steal his contentment, his testimony was powerful. Even many who belonged to Caesar's household were compelled to know Christ! (see v. 22). Paul had a secret they wanted to know.

One of these five thieves is probably working overtime on you right now. Which is being the hardest for you to guard against? What has it been taking from you? How have you been somewhat successful at standing down this particular joy snatcher?

PRAYING GOD'S WORD TODAY

I bow my knees before You, my faithful Father, from whom every family in heaven and on earth is named. I pray that You may grant me, according to the riches of Your glory, to be strengthened with power through Your Spirit in my inner man (Eph. 3:14–16), enabling me, reminding me to be steadfast, immovable, always excelling in the Lord's work, knowing that my labor in the Lord is not in vain (1 Cor. 15:58). May the peace of Christ, to which we have been called in one body, control my heart. And may I be thankful, for the glory of Your great name (Col. 3:15).

Day 82

Never Forget

BEFORE YOU BEGIN

Read 1 Timothy 1:12–17

STOP AND CONSIDER

He considered me faithful, appointing me to the ministry—one who was formerly a blasphemer, a persecutor, and an arrogant man. (vv. 12–13)

How would you describe your life before Christ intervened? If you came to Christ early in life, what are you still painfully aware that He saved you from? ______________________

____

____

What happens if we forget what we could have been had Christ not revealed Himself to us? What are the dangers of having a faulty spiritual memory? ______________________

____

____

____

Paul and Timothy spent years together, yet oddly the apostle had hardly greeted the young preacher in this first letter before he repeated his testimony. Twenty-six years had passed since a blinding light had opened the eyes of a persecutor named Saul, but he was still repeating his testimony because he never forgot. He remembered like it was yesterday.

I don't know how you feel about Paul or the journey we've shared, but I know I want his unquenchable passion! Fortunately, it's contagious. We catch it by imitating what he did to get it. I see at least six reasons in 1 Timothy 1:12–17.

1. *He never forgot the privilege of ministry* (v. 12). Unlike most of us, Paul's conversion and subsequent ministry took him from a life of relative ease to almost constant pressure and turmoil. He was beaten, stoned, whipped, jailed, and starved in the course of his ministry; yet he considered his calling to serve God to be the greatest privilege anyone could receive.

A host of reasons probably existed for Paul's continued gratitude. One possibility stands out most in my mind. His chief desire was "to know Christ" (Phil. 3:10 NIV). I believe the more he knew Christ, the more he saw His greatness. The more Paul saw His greatness, the more amazed he was to have the privilege to serve Him. We will also become more amazed over our privilege to serve as we seek to know Christ better.

2. *He never forgot who he had been* (v. 13). God used Paul to perform more wonders and birth more churches than any other human in the New Testament. In a quarter of a century, Paul had plenty of time to forget who he had been, taking pride in his powerful ministry. One reason God leaves our memories of past repented sin intact is because a twinge of memory is indeed profitable to us. Pride is the archenemy of ministry.

I think one reason Paul continued to remember who he had been was because his love for Christ continued to grow. The more he loved Christ, the more he wondered how he could have sinned against Him so horrendously in his past. I've personally experienced this. Even though I know I am fully forgiven, the deeper my love for Christ has grown, the more I regret past sins.

3. *He never forgot the abundance of God* (v. 14). Paul discovered God's intent was not just for us to get by. He is not the God of barely enough. Paul encountered a God who super-gave! Paul wrote, "The grace of our Lord overflowed, along with the faith and love that are in Christ Jesus." Paul never forgot the abundance of God. Greater still, God never forgets the abundance of our need.

He never forgot who he had been. He relished the abundance of God. He never lost sight of the basics.

Isaiah described God's devotion to His children: "Can a woman forget her nursing child, or lack compassion for the child of her womb? Even if these forget, yet I will not forget you" (Isa. 49:15). He sees our needs like a mother sees her helpless infant's needs. Like a loving mother, He will never forget one of His children.

4. *He never forgot the basics* (v. 15). Can you imagine the wealth of knowledge Paul gained in his quest for God? Still he never lost sight of the most important truth he ever learned: "Christ Jesus came into the world to save sinners." May we also never forget! We don't have to lose touch with our most basic belief to press on to maturity.

How long has it been since tears stung your eyes when someone received Christ? Or how long has it been since you felt deep gratitude for the simplicity of your salvation? I beg you, never stop thanking Christ for coming into the world specifically to save you.

5. *He never forgot his primary role* (v. 16). According to the apostle, God saved "the worst" of sinners to "demonstrate the utmost patience as an example." The Greek word for "example" means "to draw a sketch or first draft as painters when they begin a picture." Paul saw himself drawn in that picture. You are painted in the portrait. I am painted in. The worst of sinners—the spiritually blind, lame, and lost—find unlimited patience in our God! If we look on the era of Paul's life and his contemporaries to be the last great movement of God, then we have tragically misunderstood. If our conclusion is "Wow! Those

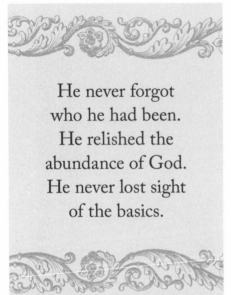

were the days," we've missed the point. God is still painting the portrait of His church. Paul was only an example of what God can do with one repentant life. God hasn't finished the picture—but one day He will.

6. *He never forgot the wonder of God* (v. 17). Twenty-six years after he fell to his knees, Paul still felt so overwhelmed by the awesome work of God that he exclaimed, "Now to the King eternal, immortal, invisible, the only God, be honor and glory forever and ever." I wish I could have seen Timothy's face while reading Paul's words. Perhaps he thought, *How has he kept his wonder?* The answer? He never forgot who he had been. He relished the abundance of God. He never lost sight of the basics.

When my oldest daughter was little and I offered her a treat that had lost its luster to her, she responded politely, "No, thank you, Mommy. I'm used to that." The apostle Paul had known Christ for twenty-six years. Still he looked back on his salvation and the privilege to serve and never got "used to that." May God grant us a memory like Paul's.

In case you've been burdened lately with the enormity of things you don't understand about God, take a moment to remember some of the basics—the things you do know. List a few here. And praise Him at each recollection. ______________________________

____

____

____

____

____

Praying God's Word Today

My precious Lord and God, just as You told Your people in an earlier day to remember that they were slaves in the land of Egypt and how You brought them out of there with a strong hand and an outstretched arm (Deut. 5:15), help me to stay keenly aware of who I was and what You have done for me. May I never forget!

Day 83

Down with Women?

Before You Begin

Read 1 Timothy 2:8–15

Stop and Consider

A woman should learn in silence with full submission. I do not allow a woman to teach or to have authority over a man; instead, she is to be silent. (vv. 11–12)

I probably don't have to ask you what your first impression is after reading the above verse. But I'll ask anyway. What do you think? ______________________________

____

____

What does it tell you about God to see that His Word was engaged with the current, hot-button issues of first-century life and culture? ______________________________

____

____

____

Glancing through the book of 1 Timothy, you'll notice a continuing exhortation for order in the churches. In stressing this, Paul made some statements about women that raise controversy. Although he used far more ink to address deacons and overseers, I don't want to be charged with cowardice by omitting any mention of his instructions to women.

When he said, "A woman should learn in silence," he did not use a Greek word that meant "complete silence or no talking. [He used a word] used elsewhere to mean settled down, undisturbed, not unruly."[16] Paul's primary ministry was geared toward Gentiles who had never been trained to have respect and reverence in worship. Paul encouraged women to observe traditional customs lest the young churches suffer a bad reputation.

The Christian movement was new and fragile. Any taint of adverse publicity could greatly hinder the mission of the church and mean persecution for believers. Women had to restrain their new freedom in Christ (Gal. 3:28) so as not to impede the progress of the gospel. Paul's "weaker brother" principle (1 Cor. 8:9) applies, where he said, "Be careful that this right of yours in no way becomes a stumbling block to the weak." Thus, women were to learn quietly, without calling attention to themselves.

In regard to instructing women not to teach men, you must understand that most women in Paul's day were illiterate. They were not taught in synagogue schools or trained by a rabbi. Paul goes on to say in verse 12 that women should not usurp authority over men. The Greek word *authenteo*, "one who claims authority," is used only this one time in the Greek translation of the Bible. This word refers to an autocrat or dictator. Paul says women were not to come in and take over!

We cannot regard verses 11 and 12 as a prohibition against women opening their mouths in church or men learning anything biblical from women. For instance, Paul gave instructions for how women are to pray and prophesy (1 Cor. 11:5). He was fully aware of Priscilla's role in teaching Apollos in Ephesus (Acts 18:26). Paul issued differing instructions for churches based on their cultural settings and his desire for order in the church.

Praying God's Word Today

Father, I am so grateful to realize that we are not following cleverly contrived myths when we consider the message of our Lord Jesus Christ; instead, we find proof in Your Word from those who were eyewitnesses of His majesty (2 Pet. 1:16). Yet, Lord, Paul speaks things in his letters that are hard to understand—things that the untaught and unstable twist to their own destruction, as they also do with the rest of the Scriptures (2 Pet. 3:16). When I am troubled by matters I don't completely understand, may I trust that Your Word is as real and relevant today as ever, and that underneath it all, there is no Jew or Greek, slave or free, male or female; for we are all one in Christ Jesus (Gal. 3:28)—all who have called upon Your name for salvation.

Day 84

Good Things to Do

Before You Begin

Read 1 Timothy 4:6–16

Stop and Consider

Practice these things; be committed to them,
so that your progress may be evident to all. (v. 15)

Many people view Christianity as if it has nothing but an inward personality. But ours is an active faith. What are some things you love to see yourself (and other believers) doing?

Spiritual growth isn't often something you can see as it's happening. But what are some of your indicators that tell you you're gaining strength, that you're starting to "get" this?

Midway through my preparation for writing this book, I began to realize that one of God's priority goals is to raise up and encourage passionate, persevering servants who are completely abandoned to His will. Paul's exhortations to Timothy stand as timeless words of advice to every servant of the living God, regardless of generation or gender. I'd like to look at a few of these today, a few more tomorrow.

"Train yourself in godliness" (v. 7). Godliness does not instantly accompany salvation. Remember, salvation is a gift. Godliness is a pursuit. The word meaning "to train" is *gumnazo*, from which we derive the word "gymnasium." The apostle drew a parallel between an athlete preparing for the Greek games and a believer pursuing godliness. An athlete who is preparing for intense competition makes frequent visits to the gym.

"Be an example" (v. 12). Although Timothy was young, Paul exhorted him not to let others who were older intimidate him. Rather, he should set an example "in conduct, in love, in faith, in purity." God is practical. His Word works. He wants us to be living proof by our example. If we're leading but we're not closely following Christ, we are misleading.

"Do not neglect the gift that is in you" (v. 14). When we receive Christ, God gives us spiritual gifts, but they must then be developed, cared for, and cultivated. For example, I received Christ as a young child, but I did not use the gift of teaching until I became an adult. Then God opened a door for me to teach Sunday school. Although He gave me the spiritual gift and opened the door for me to use it, God expected me to accept the opportunity and fan the gift into a flame. Every week I had to study. I also spent numerous hours listening to other teachers. I asked one to disciple me personally. I had to develop a consistent prayer life. I also had to learn from my blunders and lessons that flopped! Still I kept asking God to teach me His Word so I could be obedient. These are a few ways God directed me to fan into flame one gift He gave me. God honors a beautiful blend of gift and grit! He gives the gift, and He expects us to have the grit to practice and learn how to use it effectively.

PRAYING GOD'S WORD TODAY

Lord, You have given me so many encouragements to help me experience life with You to the full, to grow with You beyond measure. You tell me to rejoice always, to pray constantly, to give thanks in everything, for this is Your will for me in Christ Jesus. But best of all, You comfort me in the knowledge that You, the God of peace, will Yourself sanctify me completely, that my spirit, soul, and body will be kept sound and blameless for the coming of our Lord Jesus Christ. For even when I am faithless, You are faithful, Lord. Having called me, You are certain to do what You have promised (1 Thess. 5:16–18, 23–24).

Day 85

Fit Behavior

Before You Begin

Read 1 Timothy 5:19–25

Stop and Consider

Some people's sins are evident, going before them to judgment. . . . Likewise, good works are obvious, and those that are not obvious cannot remain hidden. (vv. 24–25)

Perhaps your hard work at godly living is going unnoticed or getting you treated like a doormat. What do you take from Paul's counsel that godliness "cannot remain hidden"?

If purity in your speech and behavior has been a particularly daunting battle lately, what might the Lord be telling you by allowing this to be a daily struggle?

We spent some time yesterday looking at several imperatives for strong ministry that Paul identified for Timothy. Today we consider two others that were part of his instruction to his son in the faith.

"Keep yourself pure" (5:22). Nothing marks the erosion of character or has the potential to destroy ministries and testimonies like impurity. Paul told Timothy to "keep" himself pure. The original word for "keep" comes from the word *teros*, meaning "a warden or guard." Paul told Timothy to stand as a guard over purity in his own life. I must take responsibility for purity in my life. You must take responsibility for purity in your life. If you are trying to keep yourself pure but you continue to fall, I encourage you to seek godly counsel. A mature and discerning believer can help you identify reasons why you continue to be drawn to impurity. It is not too late to consecrate your life to God and find victory.

"Turn away from godless chatter" (6:20 NIV). The word for "godless" is *bebelos*, which speaks of "a threshold, particularly of a temple." This "threshold" separates the profane from the holy. If we are believers in Christ, we are sacred temples of His Holy Spirit. We have a choice as to what crosses the threshold and finds a place in our temples. Paul exhorts believers to discern a line in conversation that should not be crossed.

Sometimes we have to think of ways to turn away from godless chatter without deeply offending another person or disrespecting someone in authority. Pursuing godliness isn't always pleasant. Sometimes we are forced to make difficult decisions. He will direct us how to turn away appropriately. If we turn away proudly and self-righteously, we ourselves have crossed an important threshold. Humility is the earmark of God's genuine servant. Even when we turn away, we should be humble.

I pray that Paul's life has compelled you to be an active part of God's agenda. I hope you will never again be satisfied to sit on the sidelines. I pray that you desire for your life to leave footprints someone else could follow straight to Christ. None of these things will happen accidentally or coincidentally. Godliness and effective ministry take attention, but nothing you could pour your energies into will ever have a greater payoff.

Praying God's Word Today

Victorious God, I thank You and boldly claim that although I am walking in the flesh, I do not wage war in a fleshly way, since the weapons of my warfare are not fleshly, but are powerful through God for the demolition of strongholds. Therefore, I demolish arguments and every high-minded thing that is raised up against the knowledge of God, taking every thought captive to the obedience of Christ (2 Cor. 10:3–5), living in the purity that You have equipped and empowered me to experience. Bless Your all-sufficient name!

Day 86

Listen Up

BEFORE YOU BEGIN

Read Titus 2:1–3

STOP AND CONSIDER

Older women are to be reverent in behavior, not slanderers,
not addicted to much wine. They are to teach what is good. (v. 3)

Who have been some of the most influential people in your life—individuals who took the time to speak into your heart and call you to noble things? ____________________

____

____

What are some of the most memorable things they have taught you? What are some of the statements they've made that continue to guide your life? ____________________

____

____

____

I wish I had the space to share about the older women who have mentored me as a Christian woman, wife, mother, and servant of God. If you are fortunate to have benefited from some godly mentors, you know that none of them were in your life accidentally. God brought you into their sphere of influence to fulfill His purposes. Paul, in his charge to older women, points out certain qualifications for a mentor to younger women.

1. *Reverent in the way she lives.* Her actions are to be those of a woman who respects God. Each of the women who have mentored me were quite different in personality, but they all shared one common denominator: their lives were replete with a reverence for God. Those I respect most are those who respect God.

2. *Not slanderous.* I believe older women may have more opportunities to remain active today than in Paul's day. One of my eighty-three-year-old friends told me one day that she was too busy to die! Still, for some who have grown idle, slanderous talk can become a means to keep life interesting. Younger women struggle with temptation to slander too. Slanderous people thrive on conflict and division. The godly mentor sets an example by edifying others through her speech—rejoicing over their victories and hurting with them in defeat.

3. *Not addicted to much wine.* The original word for "addicted" is *douloo*, meaning "to enslave." In Paul's generation, wine was the primary substance to which a woman might become addicted. Today we could fill a grocery aisle with potentially enslaving substances. I have two very dear friends whose mothers were alcoholics. They still struggle with the painful results. So many people in our society are enslaved to different substances. Alcohol, prescription and nonprescription drugs, diet pills, sleeping pills, and illegal drugs are readily available to anyone the least bit desperate or vulnerable.

The general purpose for older women mentoring younger women is stated at the end of Titus 2:3: "to teach what is good." The original Greek word for "good" is *kalos*, which "expresses beauty as a harmonious completeness, balance, proportion." Older women are to teach younger women about genuine beauty: God's idea of a beautiful woman.

Praying God's Word Today

You have taught us in Your Word, Lord, that people fall without guidance, but with many counselors there is deliverance (Prov. 11:14). Plans fail when there is no counsel, but with many advisers they succeed (Prov. 15:22). I ask You to line my path with people who speak the truth, and may my ears be open to discern Your wisdom.

Day 87

Family Matters

Before You Begin

Read Titus 2:4–5

Stop and Consider

Encourage the young women to love their husbands and children,
to be sensible, pure, good homemakers, and submissive to their husbands. (vv. 4–5)

Think through the various concerns you have as a wife and mother. How has God been calling you to take responsibility for improving your part in these relationships?

What would be some of the most delightful, positive results in your home if you could stay mindful of these instructions from Titus 2?

In his letter to Titus, Paul mentions three distinct ways in which older women are to help younger women. Let's see what we can learn from these.

1. *Love your husband.* Interestingly, the original word used for "love" is not *agape* this time. It's *philandros*, which speaks of "loving [someone] as a friend." Romantic love is so important in a marriage, but we also need to learn to be a friend to our mates. Women often have several good friends, but men tend to have fewer close friendships. A man often needs his wife to be a friend as well as a lover. *Phileo* love, which is central to *philandros*, grows from common interests. By our feminine natures, women don't often share the same interests as men. But we can learn to share their interests! I want to be a better friend to my husband. If you're married, let's make this commitment together. We can be a friend to our spouses. Let's start working on it right away.

2. *Love your children.* You may be thinking, *Who needs to be taught how to love her children?* Lots of wounded people, that's who. I would make four suggestions to those who have difficulty loving their children: 1) Seek a mentor who can help train you to be a loving parent. 2) Seek sound, godly counsel to discover why your heart is hindered and how you can find freedom in Christ. 3) *Do* the right things until you *feel* the right things. In other words, hug your children and tell them you love them whether or not these actions come easily for you. 4) Take up your children's interests. Attend their school functions, go to their games, have their friends over for pizza! Hang in there and seek some good support!

3. *Be busy at home.* The original word for "busy" means "one who looks after domestic affairs with prudence and care." I believe Paul wanted older women to teach younger women that homes and families do not take care of themselves. Someone has to watch over the priorities. Children don't raise themselves. Someone has to watch over them and be involved. A marriage doesn't improve itself. Someone has to watch over it and encourage growth and intimacy. Even if we work, wise women still remain very involved in their homes and families. The wife and mother has something to give her home and family that no one else can supply as effectively: tenderness, nurturing, a personal touch.

Praying God's Word Today

O Father, how I long to be obedient and purposeful in all things, especially in the sphere of my home and family, where You have called me to open my mouth with wisdom and to speak loving instruction from my tongue, to watch over the activities of my household and not to be idle (Prov. 31:26–27). Strengthen me, Lord, to be faithful, to be patient, and to live with integrity of heart in my house (Ps. 101:2). I need Your help. I want Your way.

Day 88

Nearing the End

Before You Begin

Read 2 Timothy 2:1–13

Stop and Consider

Keep in mind Jesus Christ, risen from the dead. . . . For this I suffer, to the point of being bound like a criminal; but God's message is not bound. (vv. 8–9)

This second letter to Timothy was written from a point of extreme physical misery in Paul's life. How do you tend to communicate when you are in a season of real suffering?

How do we keep it possible to think deep thoughts and to talk about significant things even when life's hardest pressures are not right on top of us?

We now approach the final letter from the pen of the apostle Paul. He wrote his second letter to Timothy during his last imprisonment in Rome, shortly before his death. Our goal is to capture the state of mind and physical conditions of the great apostle in the final season of his life. The letter reveals several descriptions of Paul's condition and state of mind during his final imprisonment.

1. *He was in physical discomfort.* Some criminals were simply incarcerated behind locked doors with no chains. Paul was held under conditions like those of a convicted killer, bound by heavy chains—the type that bruise and lacerate the skin. He was almost sixty years old and had taken enough beatings to make him quite arthritic. The lack of mobility greatly intensified any ailments or illnesses. He most likely was reduced to skin and bones. The cells where the worst prisoners were chained were usually filthy, wet, and rodent-infested dungeons. The beauty and articulation of Paul's final letter cannot be fully appreciated without realizing how physically uncomfortable he must have been when he wrote it.

2. *He was probably humiliated.* Captors in ancient prisons often thought of ways to shame their captives. Perhaps the least of their inhumanities was not allowing prisoners to wash and dress themselves adequately. Their confines doubled as bedroom and bathroom. In 2 Timothy 1:12, Paul said, "That is why I suffer these things. But I am not ashamed." Paul's words may hint at the attempts of his captors to shame him. He told Timothy several times not to be ashamed of him. As much as Paul had suffered, he was unaccustomed to the treatment he received in the final season of his life.

3. *He felt deserted and lonely.* No one came forward at Paul's first hearing. Can you imagine the loneliness he must have experienced as the bailiff called for defense witnesses, and silence fell over the courtroom? I don't think they deserted him because they didn't love him. Many grieved because they did not come to his defense, but they were frightened for their lives. As far as most of them were concerned, Paul was on death row anyway. They couldn't save him. After all, he was certainly guilty of denying the deity of Nero. Even in these extreme straits Paul still said, "May it not be counted against them" (4:16).

4. *He longed for normalcy.* Although Paul's life was seldom normal in our terms, I believe he longed in his last season for things that were normal to him. He wanted his oldest friends. He asked for Mark. He spoke of Luke at his side. He sent greetings to Priscilla and Aquila. He begged Timothy to come quickly. His request for his scrolls, especially the parchments, also tenders my heart. His scrolls were probably copies of Old Testament Scriptures. Very likely he had also recorded on parchments facts about the earthly life of Christ, based on the stories of Peter and Luke.

Paul's sanity was protected by his certainty. He knew the One in whom he had believed.

I can't begin to put myself in Paul's position, but if I were away from loved ones and facing certain death, I would want several things. I have stacks of journals where I've recorded prayers too private to allow anyone to read, yet I cannot bring myself to throw them away. During uncertain times when I'm called to walk by faith, I can turn back to my personal records of God's faithfulness and find strength again. My Bible and my journals are my most treasured tangible belongings. During difficult days, even holding my Bible close to my chest brings me comfort. No doubt Paul longed for these things.

A person confined and facing death inevitably turns the mental pages of the past. Surely Paul was no different. He must have thought about Tarsus. His mother's face. His father's voice. His childhood in a Jewish community. His first impressions of Jerusalem. The classroom debates he enjoyed. The way people whispered about his genius behind his back. His bright future. His return to Tarsus and the respect he commanded. His drive to persecute the people of the Way. The blinding light that sent him to his knees. He traded a life of respect and honor for one of rejection and tribulation. If his childhood friends could have seen him in that horrendous dungeon, they might have surmised that he had traded everything for nothing.

So, what do you have when you have nothing left? You have what you know. Faced with humiliation, Paul proclaimed, "But I am not ashamed, because I know whom I have believed and am persuaded that He is able to guard what has been entrusted to me until that day" (1:12). Paul's sanity was protected by his certainty. He knew the One in whom he had believed.

Paul had entrusted everything to Christ. No matter how difficult circumstances grew, he never tried to take it back. As the chains gripped his hands and feet and the stench of death assailed him, he recalled everything he had entrusted to his Savior. With chained hands, Paul could still touch the face of God.

Paul was obviously kept going by his complete confidence in God. He had seen enough over the years to be absolutely certain that his life was invested in the most secure asset imaginable. How can you apply this confidence to your current life situation?

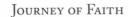

Praying God's Word Today

Precious Father, we are always confident and know that while we are at home in the body we are away from You—for we walk by faith, not by sight—yet we are confident and satisfied to be out of the body and at home with You. Therefore, whether we are at home or away, we make it our aim to be pleasing to You (2 Cor. 5:6–9). We make it our aim to want nothing *but* You.

Day 89

Death and Other Facts of Life

BEFORE YOU BEGIN

Read 2 Timothy 4:9–18

STOP AND CONSIDER

The Lord will rescue me from every evil work and will bring me safely into His heavenly kingdom. To Him be the glory forever and ever! (v. 18)

What are some of the "evil works" you're looking forward to leaving behind at your death? Name some of the other sheer reliefs that will finally be ours when we're with Jesus.

Eternal life would be sweet all by itself. But how is the Christian's hope intensified by knowing that eternal life is the gift of a loving Father who wants us that close, that long?

Paul knew without a doubt he was soon to die. Yet he was no masochist. He wasn't begging for the guillotine. He simply looked at life through the window of these words: "For to me, to live is Christ and to die is gain" (Phil. 1:21 NIV). Our entire journey together has been an effort to study the heart of a man who could sincerely make such a statement. Christ had profoundly transformed Paul's attitude toward life and death.

1. *Paul saw death as a departure.* He did not say, "The time for my death is close." He said, "The time for my departure is close" (2 Tim. 4:6). His entire life was a series of departures. He followed the leading of the Spirit through Judea, Syria, Cilicia, Galatia, Pamphylia, Asia, Macedonia, Achaia, and Italy. He never knew what awaited him as he entered a city, but one result was inevitable—as surely as he arrived, he would depart. God never let him hang his hat for long. "Our citizenship is in heaven," he had said (Phil. 3:20). To him, settling in would be pointless until then. Paul had faithfully done his time in Rome and, predictably, another departure awaited him. This time, he was going home.

2. *Paul saw death as a rescue.* Paul didn't see death as a defeat. He did not believe the enemy finally had his way. He saw death as a rescue! We tend to define the word "rescue" an entirely different way. God certainly rescued Paul many times on this earth, just as He has rescued us, yet Paul knew the greatest rescue of all awaited him. Death was not God's refusal to act; death was God's ultimate rescue. Oh, if we could only understand this difficult truth, how different our perspectives would be. Paul not only saw death as the ultimate rescue from evil; he saw death as a rescue from frail, limited bodies.

3. *Paul saw death as a safe passage.* Remember the words of 2 Timothy 4:18. God will not only rescue us, but He will bring us safely to His heavenly kingdom. Earlier we learned the original Greek meaning for the word "rescue." *Rhuomai* means "to draw or snatch from danger, rescue, deliver. This is more with the meaning of drawing to oneself than merely rescuing for someone or something." God is not simply trying to snatch us from danger. He desires to draw us to Himself spiritually, then one day physically. When our ultimate rescue comes, God's purpose is to deliver us to Himself—safely.

Praying God's Word Today

Lord Jesus, You have assured us not to let our hearts be troubled, for in our Father's house are many dwelling places; if not, You would have told us. You declare that You have gone away to prepare a place for us, and that You will come back and receive us to Yourself, so that where You are, we may be also (John 14:1–3). Therefore, I receive the peace You have left with us—Your peace that You have given to us. I will not let my heart be troubled or fearful since I know that You do not give to us as the world gives (John 14:27). I know that You will care for me—and, yes, even use me for Your glory—all the way to the very end.

Day 90

The Good Fight

BEFORE YOU BEGIN

Read 2 Timothy 4:1–8

STOP AND CONSIDER

I am already being poured out as a drink offering, and the time for my departure is close. I have fought the good fight, I have finished the race, I have kept the faith. (vv. 6–7)

What's keeping you from doing battle in these last days? How many more victories are you willing to forfeit to the enemy of fatigue?

What would you like to see issue forth from your life before the Lord declares that your race is finished?

Paul wasn't just pulling a word picture out of a hat when he uttered the statement, "I have fought the good fight, I have finished the race, I have kept the faith" (2 Tim. 4:7). Anyone in the Roman Empire would know exactly what he was talking about. I wouldn't be the least bit surprised, in fact, if these words spread and ultimately hastened his death.

In AD 67, the year of Paul's death, Nero had the audacity to enter himself in the Olympic games. Mind you, Olympic athletes trained all their lives for the games. The thirty-year-old, soft-bellied emperor used medications to induce vomiting rather than exercise to control his weight.[17] He was in pitiful shape and ill prepared, but who would dare tell him he could not compete? He cast himself on a chariot at Olympia and drove a ten-horse team. "He fell from the chariot and had to be helped in again; but, though he failed to stay the course and retired before the finish, the judges nevertheless awarded him the prize."[18]

Nero did not finish the race. Nevertheless, a wreath was placed on his head, and he was hailed the victor. He showed his gratitude for their cooperation in the ridiculous scam by exempting Greece from taxation. For his processional entry into Rome he chose the chariot Augustus had used in his triumph in a former age, and he wore a Greek mantle spangled with gold stars over a purple robe. The Olympic wreath was on his head. "Victims were sacrificed in his honour all along the route."[19] You can be fairly certain they were from a despised group of people commonly called *Chrestiani*, or Christians.

Needless to say, word of the humiliating victory spread faster than the fire of AD 64. Soon after Nero returned to Rome, the apostle wrote his stirring final testimony. The edict was signed for his execution.

Yet God did not allow the deaths of His beloved apostles to overshadow their lives. Their departures were intimate encounters between themselves and the One for whom they laid down their lives. Teaching handed down through the ages tells us two soldiers by the name of Ferega and Parthemius brought Paul word of his death. They approached him and asked for his prayers that they might also believe in his Christ. Having received life from his instruction, they then led Paul out of the city to his death.[20] Traditional teaching claims he prayed just before his execution. At this point I would have trouble believing anything different. Wouldn't you?

> May God find us faithful, unstoppable servants of the One who saved us, waiting to hang our hats on heaven's door.

After praying, the apostle Paul gave his neck to the sword. But before his earthly tent had time to collapse to the ground, his feet stood on holy ground. His eyes, possibly scarred and blurred from a glorious light on a Damascus road, saw their first crystal-clear vision in thirty years. Paul himself had written, "For now we see indistinctly, as in a mirror, but then face to face" (1 Cor. 13:12). Faith became sight, and the raptured saint saw Christ's face. He beheld the ultimate surpassing glory.

No thought of beatings. No questions of timing. No pleas for vengeance. No list of requests. Just the sight of unabashed, unhindered, unveiled glory. And he had not yet looked past His face—"God's glory in the face of Jesus Christ" (2 Cor. 4:6). He was seeing the face he had waited thirty years to see. The Righteous Judge raised a wreath of righteousness and placed it on the head of His faithful servant. He had finished the race. And more impressively, he had kept the faith. Never doubt the difference.

Paul once wrote, "Now I know in part, but then I will know fully, as I am fully known" (1 Cor. 13:12). The partial knowledge of Christ that Paul had acquired in his lifetime was the same knowledge he claimed to be worth every loss (see Phil. 3:8–10). Oh, my friend, if partial knowledge of the Lord Jesus is worth every loss, what then will full knowledge be like? I cry out with our brother Paul, "Oh, the depth of the riches both of the wisdom and the knowledge of God!" (Rom. 11:33). One day the prayer of the apostle will be answered for all of us. We will indeed "grasp how wide and long and high and deep is the love of Christ . . . and know this love that surpasses knowledge" (Eph. 3:18–19 NIV).

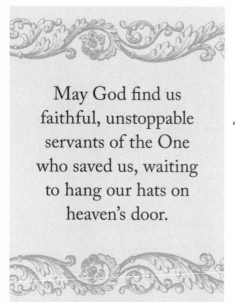

Until then, may God find us faithful, unstoppable servants of the One who saved us, waiting to hang our hats on heaven's door. "For I am persuaded that neither death nor life, nor angels nor rulers, nor things present, nor things to come, nor powers, nor height, nor depth, nor any other created thing will have the power to separate us from the love of God that is in Christ Jesus our Lord!" (Rom. 8:38–39).

Most Worthy Lord,
make me a drink offering
and take me not home
until the cup is overturned
the glass broken
and every drop loosed
for Your glory.

What's the next thing you'll do or think or approach differently, based on what you've seen in the apostle Paul's life? ____________________

Praying God's Word Today

Knowing the time, Lord, I know that it is already the hour for me to wake up from sleep, for my salvation is nearer than when I first believed. The night is nearly over, and the daylight is near. So help me discard the deeds of darkness and put on the armor of light. Help me walk with decency, as in the daylight: not in carousing and drunkenness, not in sexual impurity and promiscuity, not in quarreling and jealousy. May I instead put on the Lord Jesus Christ, and make no plans to satisfy the fleshly desires (Rom. 13:11–14). As it was for Paul, may it also be for me—that I will never boast about anything except Your cross, Lord Jesus, through whom the world has been crucified to me, and I to the world (Gal. 6:14). Praise You, Lord. Praise You now. Praise You forever.

Notes

1. Rabbi Solomon Ganzfried, trans. Hyman E. Goldin, *Code of Jewish Law* (New York: Hebrew Publishing Company, 1993), I, 1.
2. Ibid., IV, 43.
3. Ibid., IV, 44.
4. Ibid., II, 62.
5. Ibid., I, 27.
6. F. B. Meyer, *Paul, A Servant of Jesus Christ* (Fort Washington, Penn.: Christian Literature Crusade, 1995), 26.
7. Ernle Bradford, *Paul the Traveller* (New York: Barnes & Noble, 1993), 35.
8. Ibid., 35.
9. Cited in Joan Comay, *Who's Who in the Old Testament* (Crown Publishers, 1980), 322.
10. Patrick Johnstone, *Operation World* (Grand Rapids, Mich.: Zondervan Publishing House, 1993), 643.
11. Trent Butler, et al., eds., *Holman Bible Dictionary* (Nashville: Holman Bible Publishers, 1991), 406.
12. Bradford, 196.
13. John F. Walvoord and Roy B. Zuck, eds., *The Bible Knowledge Commentary New Testament* (Wheaton, Ill.: Victor Books, 1983), 421.
14. Ibid., 422.
15. Ibid., 640.
16. Ibid., 735.
17. Robert Graves, *The Twelve Caesars* (New York: Penguin Books, 1957), 222.
18. Ibid., 226.
19. Ibid., 226.
20. John Foxe, *Foxe's Book of Martyrs* (New Kensington, Penn.: Whitaker House, 1981), 12.